They were inside the tomb . . .

As Ricky stepped next to the vault, he tried to hold the flashlight steady. He didn't want his nervousness to shake the beam of light. He closed his eyes until he could barely see and aimed the flashlight into the vault.

"How dare you!"

From inside the tomb a deep throaty voice cut through the howling wind outside. Each word dripped with anger.

The boys jumped from fright and wheeled around. "Who said that?" Ricky fearfully asked as he waved his flashlight throughout the tomb.

"Look! Over there!" shouted Tyler, pointing to the corner by the door. "It's — it's the ghost!"

The Haunted Graveyard

And Other True Ghost Stories

ALLAN ZULLO

Rainbow Bridge®
Troll

To Beth Spicer, for her spirited efforts in caring for the little goblins and one big ghoul that haunt her house.

Contents of this edition copyright © Troll Communications L.L.C.
Watermill Press is an imprint and registered trademark of
Troll Communications L.L.C.

Copyright © 1996 by The Wordsellers, Inc.
Published by Rainbow Bridge, an imprint and trademark of Troll
Communications L.L.C. All rights reserved. No part of this book may
be reproduced or utilized in any form or by any means, electronic or
mechanical, including photocopying, recording, or by any information
storage and retrieval system, without written permission from the
publisher.

Cover design by Tony Greco & Associates.
Cover illustration by Kersti Frigell.

Printed in the United States of America.

10   9   8   7   6   5   4

Library of Congress Cataloging-in-Publication Data

Zullo, Allan.
The haunted graveyard and other true ghost stories / Allan Zullo.
p.   cm.
"Rainbow Bridge."
Summary: Ten stories, taken from the files of noted ghost hunters,
describing hauntings of everything from caves to big city apartments.
ISBN 0-8167-3825-4 (pbk.)
1. Ghost—Juvenile literature.   [1. Ghosts.]   I. Title.
BF1461.Z85   1996   133.1—dc20   95-14798

CONTENTS

DO YOU BELIEVE IN GHOSTS?

Some kids claim they have seen ghosts. Other kids say they've actually been haunted by them.

In many cases, experts were called in to investigate these so-called hauntings. Usually, the experts walked away baffled. All they knew for sure was that something weird had happened that could not fully be explained.

This book is a chilling collection of stories about spirits haunting everything from graveyards to a cave to a big-city apartment. You'll read ten spine-tingling tales inspired, in part, by real-life cases taken from the files of noted ghost hunters. The names and places in the stories have been changed to protect everyone's privacy.

Do you believe in ghosts? You might after reading the spooky stories in this book!

THE HAUNTED GRAVEYARD

"So, do you want to do it?" Tyler Mathews asked with a sly grin.

"I'm game if you are," replied his best friend, Ricky Hernandez.

"Then it's set. Tomorrow night we're going to sneak into the tomb and prove that the ghost of Sarah Winslow exists!"

The site where the two 13-year-olds planned to carry out their creepy mission was a large grim-looking tomb that loomed in the middle of Greenwood Cemetery. The rectangular-shaped chamber—the size of a one-car garage—stood 10 feet (3 m) high and had thick outside walls of gray granite stained by years of city grime. Below the flat roof the east and west walls had horizontal openings three feet (1 m) wide and a foot (.3 m) deep, allowing the morning and afternoon sun to fall on the vault inside.

The tomb stood out from all the other memorials in the cemetery. Above the main chamber rose a 20-foot- (6-m-) tall dull black marble spire the shape of the Washington Monument. Another unique feature was the entrance. It had a padlocked wrought-iron door encased in Plexiglas so passersby could look inside at the vault that contained the casket of Sarah Winslow.

Sarah was an heiress to a fortune made from a perfume company. A strange woman, Sarah kept to herself and guarded her privacy, yet she donated huge sums of money for a building, a park, and a hospital wing on the condition that they be named after her.

Ever since the boys could remember, there was talk that Sarah Winslow's ghost could be seen pacing back and forth inside her tomb late at night. For years kids would sneak into the cemetery, stand outside the see-through door of the tomb, and wait with tingling anticipation for a sign of the phantom. Some claimed to have seen a misty figure float inside, but no one really believed the kids because they never presented any proof.

Tyler and Ricky planned to get the evidence that would make them heroes in the eyes of their friends. The boys were going to attempt a scheme that no one else in the neighborhood had the guts to try—sneak *inside* the tomb.

"I've got it figured out," Tyler told Ricky. "The padlock on the door is old and rusty. A few swift hits with my hammer, and it will break. Then we go inside and wait for the ghost to appear. And when she does, we're prepared."

"Right," said Ricky, holding up his camera. "I've got ultra-high-speed film, so I can shoot the ghost without a flash. Once I take the pictures, we're out of there."

On Saturday Ricky went over to Tyler's house to spend the

night. After Tyler's mother had gone to bed at about 11:30 P.M., the boys slipped out the back door and walked two blocks to the cemetery.

As they reached the locked gate to the graveyard, they heard the rumbling sound of distant thunder. "Looks like a storm is brewing," said Tyler.

The boys scaled the four-foot- (1.2-m-) high stone wall that surrounded the cemetery and jumped down to the other side. "Is this cool or what?" whispered Tyler, his eyes dancing with excitement. "It's midnight and we're in the 'bone yard,' the 'marble orchard,' the place where hundreds of dead people are taking an 'earth bath.'"

"That's sick."

"Yeah, I know," Tyler said with a wink.

They crouched down low and quietly walked toward the imposing Winslow tomb. As they weaved their way around old tombstones, markers, and freshly dug graves, Ricky started feeling a little queasy. But he didn't dare show it to Tyler for fear of being called a wimp.

When they reached the tomb, the boys peeked through the Plexiglas door. Ricky turned on the flashlight and scanned the inside. It looked spookier at night than it did during the day. A thin shaft of light from a street lamp cast an eerie glow onto the vault.

"Are you ready?" whispered Tyler. Ricky nodded. Tyler pulled out his hammer and hit the rusty padlock. The clang echoed off the gravestones.

"Shhh," said Ricky. "You're going to wake up the dead."

"Hey, do you want to break in or not?" asked Tyler, getting slightly annoyed.

"Yeah, I do."

"Okay, then, let me hammer." After a few more whacks, the old padlock broke. "Success!" With the broken lock dangling from the door, they crept inside the tomb. Their noses soon twitched from the musty smell of mildew.

Ricky moved the flashlight around the chamber. Two tall clay pots with plastic flowers stood on both sides of the entrance. A wooden bench leaned against the east wall. On the opposite wall was a portrait of Sarah Winslow made from small colored ceramic tiles. At the back of the tomb on a raised cement platform rested the marble vault that held her remains. Carved in fancy script on the side was the name *Sarah Elizabeth Winslow* and the words *Rest in Peace.*

Ricky went up to the vault and lightly rubbed his fingers across the lid. It felt cold to the touch even though it was a warm muggy summer night. A chill snaked across his shoulders. *I really don't want to be here right now. This was a dumb idea. What if we get caught? What if the police think we're body snatchers? What if we really do see a ghost? What if . . .*

SLAM!

The boys jerked around and saw that the door had shut with a loud bang.

"The wind must have closed it," Tyler said with a nervous laugh. He walked over to push the door open, but it wouldn't budge. He tried jiggling the handle and ramming the door with his shoulder. Nothing worked.

"I—I don't understand," stammered Tyler. "The door is locked!"

"Quit joking around," said Ricky. "I know you're trying to scare me, but I'm on to you."

"This is no joke!" Tyler snapped, his voice rising with anxiety. "See for yourself."

When Ricky's efforts failed to open the door, the two of them kicked and pounded on it to no avail. Ricky then shined his flashlight through the Plexiglas. "Tyler, look at that! The padlock is fastened back onto the door!"

"Some jerk must have followed us to the tomb and locked us in," muttered Tyler. He pounded the door in disgust. "We're trapped inside like rats."

Tyler then climbed onto the vault, leaned against the west wall, and pressed his face against the slit-shaped opening. "Hello! Hello!" he shouted. "Is anybody out there?"

Suddenly a flash of light, followed a half second later by a thunderous boom, sent Tyler reeling. He fell onto the vault and rolled off onto the hard cement floor. "Ow! That hurt!" he moaned as he picked himself up. "I just got jolted by lightning." Examining his skinned elbow and knee in the glare of Ricky's flashlight, Tyler added, "It's starting to storm outside, so no one is going to hear us yelling. I guess we'll have to stay here until morning and then shout out the window for help."

Ricky gulped. "Morning? What will your mother say when she finds out we're not home? What if she tells my parents? What if—"

"Shhh, do you hear that?"

A scraping noise that sounded like two heavy cement slabs rubbing against each other echoed from the front of the tomb. Ricky uneasily aimed the flashlight toward the vault. "I don't see anything unusual." Then his heart skipped a beat. "Uh-oh. Look at the lid!"

The granite lid to the vault had shifted slightly, exposing a few inches of the darkened space inside.

"The lid wasn't like that when we first came in here," said Tyler.

"Maybe when you climbed on top of the vault and fell off, you jarred it loose." Ricky climbed on the bench next to the east wall and yelled out the slit window, "Help! Help!"

"Save your breath, Ricky. We're stuck here."

"You don't think the ghost moved the lid, do you, Tyler?"

"Could be." Part of Tyler wished the ghost would appear, but another part hoped she wouldn't. "Well," he said with a sigh, "we came here to find a ghost. Keep your camera ready."

They hunkered on the bench with their knees up by their chins and said little to each other. Outside, the rainstorm turned fierce. Howling wind gusts swirled around the tomb, creating a dreadful shrieking sound through the slit windows. With each flash of lightning the boys winced as crashing thunder bounced off the walls in eerie echoes.

"We shouldn't have come here, Tyler," Ricky whined. "It was a stupid idea."

"Hey, nobody forced you. All week you were telling me how cool it was. And now—"

"Wait. Do you smell that?"

Tyler sniffed the air. "It's sweet and flowery, like perfume."

"Yeah, perfume." Ricky coughed. "It's getting stronger and stronger." He gagged as he waved his hands in front of his face. "Man, this stuff is making me sick."

Between coughs Tyler blurted, "Me too. Where's it coming from?"

Ricky got up and, while inhaling, walked toward the source of the smell. "It's coming from the vault!" he said.

Tyler hustled to his side. "Shine the flashlight in the vault. Let's see what's inside."

"Are you crazy? What if it's a skeleton?"

"There shouldn't be anything in the vault except the casket—and maybe the reason for the perfume smell."

As he stepped next to the vault, Ricky tried to keep his sweaty hand steady. He didn't want his nervousness to shake the beam. He closed his eyes until he could barely see and aimed the flashlight into the vault.

"How dare you!"

From inside the tomb a woman's deep throaty voice cut through the howling wind outside. Each word dripped with anger.

The boys jumped from fright and wheeled around. "Who said that?" Ricky fearfully asked as he waved his flashlight throughout the tomb.

"Look! Over there!" shouted Tyler, pointing to the corner by the door. "It's—it's the ghost!"

A faint glowing mist in the shape of a human figure hovered in front of the horror-stricken boys. They couldn't see any details of the phantom—no face or arms—but it had the shape of a woman draped in a hooded cloak.

Ricky was so shocked by what he saw that he dropped his flashlight. It struck the concrete floor, breaking the bulb, spilling the batteries, and plunging the tomb into darkness.

"How *dare* you invade my privacy, my resting place!" hissed the voice, dragging out each syllable in a spooky voice that all but squeezed the air out of the boys' lungs.

Ricky and Tyler backpedaled until their shoulders pressed up against the side of the vault. Their wide eyes remained locked on the glowing misty figure, which they could still see in the darkness.

"Answer me!" the figure commanded.

Tyler tried to speak, but nothing came out of his mouth except a little squeak. Eventually he managed to stammer, "We—we wanted to see if there was a ghost here."

"Have you no decency? No respect for the dead? Shame on you!"

"We're sorry," said Ricky. "Very, very, very sorry."

"We'd leave now, but we're locked in," Tyler explained.

"You must pay for this breach of peace!" the phantom raged before quickly fading into the darkness.

And then the torment began. The boys were jarred by a shrill, ear-piercing scream that grew louder and higher in pitch before tapering to an unearthly wail. Then it repeated again and again, coming in waves that set the boys' teeth on edge. The screams weren't from pain or anguish or even of anger. They were much worse—designed to curdle the blood.

Combined with the booming thunder and shrieking wind outside, the ghastly screams reduced the boys into trembling human balls. Down on their knees, hands over ears, the boys uttered shouts of their own in a desperate attempt to drown out the horrid screams.

Finally, after what seemed like hours, the appalling assault on their ears dwindled until the only sounds the boys heard were the storm and their own heavy breathing.

But then the boys were tormented by a different noise that had them once again covering their ears. It was the grating sound of long fingernails scraping maddeningly across a chalkboard.

"It's driving me crazy!" Ricky yelled. "Stop it! Stop it!" But the nerve-jangling noise didn't ease for another hour.

Mercifully, the tormenting sounds and the terrible storm ceased at daybreak, replaced by the gentle warbling of a flock of songbirds. Exhausted, the red-eyed, sweat-soaked boys slouched on the bench.

"We made it through the night," Ricky said wearily. "I don't know how, but we did it."

"We actually saw the ghost," murmured Tyler, almost in disbelief. "But who's going to believe us?"

"Everyone," Ricky replied. And then he broke out in a big grin and held up the camera.

"You took pictures of her?" Tyler asked in amazement.

"Yep," said Ricky proudly. "Right after I dropped the flashlight. I snapped about six photos. We've got her on film, Tyler!"

Tyler high-fived his pal and said, "Come on, let's take turns yelling for help so we can get out of here."

Ricky climbed onto the back of the bench and looked out the window slit. "Hey, I see someone!" he told Tyler. Turning back to the window, Ricky shouted, "Help! Help! Over here!"

"Who is it?" asked Tyler.

"It's the caretaker. Hey, he's walking past us. Why doesn't he look up at the window? Help! Help! Over here! Over here!"

Tyler groaned. "Yelling won't do any good. The caretaker is deaf!"

Ricky slumped back down on the bench. "I can't stand to stay here all day. I'll lose my mind. What can we do?"

Tyler pulled off his own shirt and unbuckled his belt. He slipped the belt through his shirt sleeve and then buckled it. Holding on to one end of the belt, he dropped the shirt through the window and waved it back and forth.

"It's too late," said Tyler. "The caretaker is gone. I was hoping to get his attention."

For the next two hours, the boys took turns looking for someone to walk within earshot of the tomb. Finally, at about 8 A.M., a gravedigger noticed the shirt in the window and heard the shouts. He walked up to the window and demanded, "What's going on?"

"Help!" shouted Tyler. "We're trapped inside the tomb. Get us out."

The gravedigger ran over to the entrance of the tomb and promptly opened the door with no effort at all. The boys stumbled out and clutched the man's arms. After offering several tearful thank-yous, Tyler asked the gravedigger, "How did you get us out so fast?"

"The door was unlocked, so I opened it."

Tyler and Ricky looked at each other blankly and then examined the padlock. It was dangling on the door—just the way they had left it when they first entered the tomb.

"But it was locked last night," said Ricky.

The boys then confessed to breaking into the tomb and told about the horror they endured throughout the night. The gravedigger scoffed at their ghost story, refusing to believe it. Then he chewed them out for their misdeed.

At the end of his lengthy scolding he told them, "You boys broke the law, and I should call the police. But I'll make a deal with you. I won't report you to the cops. Instead, I'll call your parents and have them pick you up. Then, for the rest of the summer, you'll help the caretaker weed around the gravestones and tend to the flowers. Now let's go to the caretaker's house."

"Wait, I forgot one thing," said Ricky. "I'll be right back." He hurried inside to get his camera, which held the proof of the Winslow tomb ghost. But moments later he came out shaking his head.

"Where's the camera?" asked Tyler.

Ricky threw up his hands in bewilderment. "I searched every square inch of the tomb. The camera is gone! We lost the only proof we had that the ghost existed."

"Hey," said Tyler, "after the night we went through, who needs any more proof?"

THE
JEALOUS GHOST

The first hint that a ghost lurked in the house came the day after Staci Ballard celebrated her 15th birthday.

Staci was home alone working on a social studies report. Her parents were out for the evening and not due back until late. Her older brother, Will, was supposed to be home by 10 P.M.

Staci closed her books, plopped on the bed, and looked at the clock. It read 9:45. Suddenly she heard the back door open and someone walk through the downstairs hall and into the kitchen. She looked out the window. Her parents' car wasn't in the driveway.

"Will, is that you?" Staci called out.

There was no answer. Just then the phone rang on the kids' line. It was Will. "Hey, Staci, I'm going to be at Mark's a little longer than I thought. If Mom and Dad get back before I do, tell them I'll be home by ten-thirty."

"Okay, wise guy," said Staci. "You're calling from the other phone line downstairs. I already heard you come home."

"Staci, I'm not in the house."

"Stop fooling with me."

"I'll prove it. Call me right back at Mark's—555-3456." Will then hung up. She dialed the number and Will answered. "See, I told you," he said. "Hey, Sis, is everything all right?"

"I think someone is in the house!" Staci gasped in alarm.

"Call 911! I'll be there in ten minutes!"

Staci gripped the phone in both hands as the dial tone hummed in her ear. She eased the receiver into its cradle, hurried to the bedroom door, and cracked it open. Footsteps squeaked on the hardwood floor in the hallway downstairs.

The back door was locked, she thought. *So if it's not Will, who's down there?* Staci crept into the upstairs hallway toward the stairs and peered over the banister. She heard the footsteps heading in her direction. The light was on in the kitchen, and Staci hoped to see at least a shadow of the figure in the hallway, but there was none. The footsteps kept advancing, slowly and steadily.

Fearfully Staci tiptoed back into her room, quietly closed the door, and locked it. The footsteps became muffled. *He must be right at the bottom of the stairs where the rug is,* she thought. The trembling girl picked up the phone and dialed 911. "There's someone in my house," she whispered. "Please send the police right now!"

Staci cowered behind the bed and waited. *That's strange,* she thought. *I don't hear anything. Stay put, Staci, don't go out there. Maybe he'll go away.*

For several agonizing minutes Staci hid in silence. Then the footsteps resumed. *He's coming up the stairs! Now he's right outside my room!* She heard two light taps on the door. Then she saw the doorknob begin to turn. Cringing in the corner, Staci frantically wondered what to do. *Dive under the bed? Hide in the closet? Make a mad dash when he breaks down the door?*

"Staci? Are you still up, honey?"

It's Mom! They're home! "Mom! Thank goodness, it's you!" Staci cried out with relief. She raced to the door, flung it open, and collapsed in her mother's arms.

"What's wrong?" asked her mother.

"There was someone in the house!"

Just then the police arrived. The officers listened to Staci's account of the intruder and fanned out through the house. They searched from the basement to the attic, shifting furniture, trunks, and boxes, and poking into dark corners with their flashlights. The windows and doors were all locked, and they found no signs of forced entry. As far as they could tell, no one had entered the house.

After the officers left, Staci felt foolish. Yet she knew that she had not imagined the incident. Someone had walked through the house.

Staci was a beautiful girl whose long, jet-black hair cascaded down to her tan shoulders. Her slender willowy build made her seem taller than she really was. Staci looked exotic because she was Amerasian—her father was American-born and her mother came from South Korea.

Popular in school, Staci had the personality and looks that guys loved. She was the first to admit that she liked to flirt and enjoyed the attention from boys. And now, best of all, she had turned 15—the age when her parents allowed her to start dating.

A day after the incident Staci was getting ready to go out with her friends. While in the bathroom she pulled her eyebrow pencil out of the drawer. It was split in two. *Oh, darn,* she thought. *How could that have happened?*

She got out a pencil sharpener and shaved the eyebrow pencil. But then, as she was darkening her eyebrows, the mirror began to mysteriously fog up. *The water isn't running in the sink, so it can't be from steam,* Staci said to herself. *I wonder why the mirror is doing that.* With her hand she tried to wipe off the mist. But seconds after she did it, the mirror fogged up again.

Staci used a washcloth to clean the mirror. When she cleared a swath, she thought she saw the reflection of a girl standing behind her. The girl looked about 15 years old. She had pale skin scarred with pockmarks, dark circles under her eyes, dirty blond hair, and a nasty scowl. Staci wheeled around, but no one was there. She looked back at the mirror, which was once again fogging up. *That's weird,* Staci thought. *Why would I imagine such a girl? And so clearly. My mind must be playing tricks on me. I wonder why.*

Staci glanced at her watch. *Oh, it's late and I'm not ready yet.* She opened a tube of lipstick and was about to apply it when she noticed that the lipstick had melted. *What's going on here? First, I find my eyebrow pencil broken, and then the mirror fogs up. Next I see a girl who isn't there, and now I find my lipstick is gooey.*

Staci found another tube in the drawer and finished doing her lips. *Well, at least the mirror isn't fogging up like before,* she thought. Staci was putting the finishing touches on her face when the mirror began to vibrate ever so slightly. Suddenly, right in front of her, a crack appeared in the upper right corner of the mirror. It slowly worked its way down in a jagged line to the lower left until it had split the glass in two.

"Mom! Dad!" Staci shouted. "Come here, quick!"

After her parents and Will rushed into the bathroom, Staci exclaimed, "Look! The mirror just cracked, and I didn't even touch it!"

"Staci, I know you're homely," Will joked. "But even I didn't know you were so ugly that you could break a mirror!"

"Oh, shut up, Will," she snapped. "It's not funny. The mirror got all fogged up, and then it started shaking and cracked. What could have caused it?"

Her father shook his head and replied, "I can't even hazard a guess."

A few nights later Staci was talking on the phone in her bedroom to Joey Villard, a boy in her history class whom she considered a dreamboat. They were discussing a chapter on explorers to the New World.

"It's kind of funny that Christopher Columbus is considered this great explorer," she said. "If you stop and think about it, he went the wrong way, landed on an island, and thought it was India!"

Joey laughed and said, "Speaking of Christopher—"

The phone crackled and buzzed. "Hello? Hello? Joey, are you still there?" asked Staci.

"Yeah, something's wrong with the line," Joey replied. "I'll call you right back."

The phone rang a few seconds later. "There, that's better," he said. "As I was saying, this Saturday Christopher Kelly is having a party and I was wondering . . ." His words were drowned out by more crackling and buzzing on the line. "So what do you think?"

"I'm sorry, Joey, I didn't hear what you said. There was noise on the line."

"I said, Chris Kelly is throwing a party Saturday, and I was hoping you'd—"

The line went dead. "Hello? Hello?" shouted Staci. She clicked the receiver button several times and then slammed the phone down in frustration. "I don't believe this. Right when I think he was going to ask me to go with him to the party!"

The phone rang again. It was Joey. "Staci?"

"Yes, it's me," she said. "Something is wrong with the phone line. It's going nuts. Anyway, you were talking about Chris Kelly's party."

"Yes, would you like to go with me? My sister has the car, and she's offered to drop us off there. I'm sure we could get a ride back."

Before Staci could answer, a girl's voice on the line hissed, "No!" And then static crackled on the line.

"Joey, are you still there?" said Staci. "Who said 'no'? I didn't say 'no.' That wasn't me. I'd love to go with you. Joey, can you hear me?" But all she heard on the other line was more static.

This is terrible, just awful, thought Staci. Quickly she thumbed through the phone directory for Joey's number. *I hope he knows it wasn't me who said no. Who was that girl?* Staci found the number and dialed Joey's line, but it was busy.

After she hung up, Staci thought, *Will! That no-good brother of mine probably did it! He pretended he was a girl.* She charged into his bedroom and demanded, "Have you been messing around with the phone while I was talking?"

Will, who was typing at his computer, looked up and replied, "No. Why?"

"Will, you and I have always had an agreement respecting each other's privacy. So help me, if I find out you were pulling some sick joke—"

"Hey, I've been working on a report. I haven't touched the phone all night."

Staci picked up the phone in Will's room. She got a dial tone and didn't hear any static, so she hurried back to her room and dialed Joey's number again. As she waited for him to pick up, she thought she heard a girl cackling in the background.

When Joey answered the phone, Staci said, "Joey, I don't know what's going on with the line, but I would love to go out with you."

"Gee, Staci, just a few minutes ago I thought I heard you say no and then hang up."

"That wasn't me. I swear. Maybe someone is fooling around with the line—"

Just then she heard a girl laughing. "Do you hear that?" Staci asked Joey.

"Hear what?"

"A girl laughing. It sounds like it's coming from far, far away. But I can hear it on the phone. She sounds mean."

"Sorry, Staci, I don't hear anything."

"Look, there's definitely something wrong with my phone. How about if we talk about the party before history class tomorrow?"

"Great, I'll see you then. Bye."

When Staci hung up the phone, she had a sickening feeling in her stomach. *Joey must think I'm a wacko. Who was that girl? And why was she trying to sabotage me?* Staci flopped onto her bed, hoping to figure out the answers.

CREAK, creak. CREAK, creak.

What's that sound? She looked around her room and gasped. The rocking chair across from her was moving slowly back and forth—on its own!

Staci gulped and, without taking her eyes off the rocker, cautiously backed away and then tore out into the hallway. "Will! Mom! Dad! Hurry over here!" They all dashed into the hallway.

"What's the matter, Staci?" asked her father.

With a trembling hand she pointed to her bedroom and said, "Look in there—and tell me what you see!"

The rest of her family carefully peered inside. Her brother and parents looked around and then at each other. "What are we supposed to see?" asked her mother.

"The rocker! It's moving by itself!"

"No, it isn't, honey."

Staci walked inside. Her mouth dropped open. "But, but, just a moment ago the rocker was moving on its own and I hadn't touched it!"

"Hmm," cracked Will. "Maybe *you're* off your rocker."

"That's enough, Will," said Staci's father.

"This isn't funny," Staci stammered. "I'm getting scared. I heard a girl's voice on the phone, and then the rocker was going on its own. The mirror, my phone, the rocker. Something eerie is going on here, and I don't know what it is."

Saturday night Staci wanted to look extra nice for Joey, who was picking her up at 8 P.M. It was her first real date and she was thrilled.

After showering, Staci began doing her hair. She turned on the blow-dryer and grabbed her favorite round brush that she used for curling and drying her hair. As she brushed her hair, it kept snagging. After struggling to untangle it, Staci noticed that many of the bristles on her brush had been ripped out. Other bristles were twisted and bent.

How did that happen? she wondered. *This is just great.* Staci was so fed up that she flung the brush against the wall. The brush bounced back and smacked her in the shin.

She found another brush and turned on the blow-dryer. But within a minute she smelled a burning odor and saw smoke curling out of the blower. She immediately unplugged it and set it down.

And then she heard a girl's chilling evil laugh. Staci spun around the bathroom. *Where's it coming from? It sounds like the girl is here with me. Must be Will watching TV.*

Staci didn't have time to be concerned. She had more important things on her mind. *Oh, no, it's 7:30. I've got to get my hair dry. No brush, no hair dryer. Look at me! I'm a mess! My hair looks like a mop! Mom doesn't have a blow-dryer. Now what am I going to do? I know. I'll call Annie.*

Staci quickly dialed her neighbor, a 25-year-old bookstore

clerk who dressed in floppy clothes, read dozens of books on unexplained phenomena, and acted like a big sister to the teen. "Annie, thank goodness you're home," said Staci. "My blow-dryer just blew up, and I don't have another one, and my hair is all wet, and Joey is coming over in a half hour. You've got to help me!"

"I'll bring my blow-dryer right over," said Annie.

"You're a lifesaver!"

A few minutes before 8 P.M., after Annie had come and gone, Staci finally finished her hair, slipped into her clothes, and then searched for her gold hoop earrings. She opened her little jewelry box and cried out in dismay. Her favorite earrings—the ones her parents bought her on her 13th birthday—were bent and twisted completely out of shape.

"Nooooo! Who is doing this?"

Before she could figure out how it happened, the doorbell rang. She peeked out the window. *It's Joey! And I'm not ready yet.* "Somebody get the door!" she yelled. Then Staci rushed into the bathroom and reached for a bottle of her favorite perfume. But in her haste it slipped through her fingers and broke. Rather than a flowery scent, the perfume reeked of rotten eggs.

Oh, yuck! I've got to get out of here. What happened to my perfume? It smells disgusting. Oh, what if I had sprayed it on me?

"Staci, get the door!" yelled Will. "I'm on the phone, and Mom and Dad are out in the backyard."

The doorbell rang again. Flustered, Staci rushed downstairs, shouting, "I'm coming!" She reached for the knob and pulled to open it. But the door wouldn't budge. After checking to make sure it was unlocked, she jerked on the handle again. But a force, like an invisible hand from behind her, was pushing against the door. Using all her might, Staci yanked on the handle. Just then the force let go and the door flew open, pitching Staci backward onto the floor.

Sitting on her rear, an embarrassed Staci looked up at Joey, who was standing outside, his eyes wide with surprise.

"Oh, hi, Joey," she said, springing to her feet and hoping her makeup covered her blushing face. *I'm going to die for sure,* she thought. *What a way to start out a date. He must think I'm such a klutz.* Staci smiled and said, "A sticky door. It's good to see you, Joey."

"Are you ready?"

"Sure am. Let's go."

They hopped in the car. As they drove off, Joey asked, "Hmm, do you smell something? Like rotten eggs?"

"Annie, what am I going to do?" asked Staci the next day when she returned the blow-dryer. "I'm freaked out over all the strange things that have happened. Last night I was a wreck, and I'm afraid Joey thinks I don't like him—but I really do. He's so nice."

"Tell me all the details, and let's see if we can figure this out," said Annie. She sipped herbal tea and listened intently as Staci recalled the bizarre incidents she had experienced.

When Staci finished, Annie announced, "I have a theory, but it's way out there." She set down her cup of tea, stared into Staci's eyes, and declared, "I think it's a ghost."

"What?"

"I think you're being haunted by a ghost!"

"That's ridiculous, Annie."

"You've seen the face of a scowling girl. You've heard a girl's mean laugh and strange footsteps. Your phone acted weird, and your rocking chair moved by itself. That's pretty strong evidence."

"Then who is this ghost? And why is it picking on me?"

Annie took a long sip from her cup. "Let's think back," she said. "The mirror, the lipstick, the eyebrow pencil, the brush, the hair dryer, the earrings, the perfume. What do they all have in common?"

"They have to do with my appearance."

"So this ghost has been trying to sabotage you—maybe because you're so pretty."

"That's silly," said Staci.

"Not really. It all ties in, especially when this ghost, which obviously is a girl, tried to mess up your date with Joey."

"Who is this ghost?"

"I think I know," replied Annie. "I'll be right back." She went into her closet and pulled out a shoe box full of photos. "One of these days I'm going to sort them out and put them in photo albums." She rifled through the photos and finally pulled one out. "Aha!" she exclaimed. "I found it! Look at this one and see if you recognize anyone besides me."

The photo showed Annie, decked out in an ankle-length red, white, and blue dress, sitting on the front stoop of Staci's house with three other girls, two of whom were waving sparklers and smiling. The third one, with short-cropped brown hair and pockmarked pale skin, sat sullenly on the steps.

"That's her!" Staci declared. "That's the face I saw in the mirror!"

"I figured you'd pick her. She's Donna Perkins. This photo was taken on the Fourth of July five years ago, two years before you and your family moved in. Donna was the Perkinses' youngest daughter, a sickly child who missed a lot of school. I felt sorry for her. She wasn't very happy, probably because she was often ill and didn't have any real friends. I never saw her running around or riding her bicycle or anything like that. Her face was all scarred from a terrible case of the chicken pox, the poor girl."

"What happened to her?" asked Staci.

"Three years ago, just before her 15th birthday, she caught a terrible fever. The next day they went into her bedroom and she was dead. I felt so sorry for her. She never went on a date, kissed a boy, or went to the prom. She didn't live long enough to do any of those things. Staci, I think the ghost of Donna Perkins has been sabotaging you."

"But why?"

"Don't you see? She was jealous. You're doing all the things she never got to do. And you're pretty!"

"I don't believe it," said Staci. "I'm being haunted by a teenage ghost who envies me. But why is she doing this to me all of a sudden?"

"Because she died just before her 15th birthday. And you just had yours." Annie downed the rest of her tea. "Well, at least we've solved the reason for the haunting. Now we've got to figure out a way to make her stop."

"I have an idea," said Staci.

That night Staci turned out all the lights in her room. Then she lit a candle and whispered, "Donna, I know you're out there. Please listen to me. Annie told me what happened to you. I feel so badly for you. But you have to understand that you are dead. We can't change that. But if you will leave me alone, and let me go on with my life without harassing me, I'll share my life with you. You can do all the things you wanted through me. Let me flirt and dance and fall in love. And every night I'll tell you about my day. So what do you say? Is it okay?"

Staci heard a noise coming from her dresser. She flicked on the light and looked around the room. Nothing was out of place, except the lid to her jewelry box was open. She looked inside.

"My earrings!" Staci shouted.

Her gold hoop earrings were back to their original shape. "So we have a deal, Donna. You and I will go through life together. We'll have a great time!"

Donna's ghost never haunted Staci again.

THE
GREATEST FEAR OF ALL

Twelve-year-old Kenny Foster kneeled down on the floor and rested his arms on the hospital bed of his grandfather Simon Bolt.

"You wanted to see me, Grandpa?"

The old man looked so frail and weak, nothing like he used to be—a muscular retired logger who loved to roughhouse with his grandkids. Simon took a deep breath from a mask connected to an oxygen tank before lifting the mask, then said, "Kenny, I don't have long to live. My days are numbered."

"Don't say that, Grandpa."

"It's a fact of life—and death," Simon said between coughs. The old man stared straight into his grandson's eyes. Kenny and Simon shared the same eye color—pale blue with a hint of hazel around the pupils. The two also shared a special bond that made Kenny the favorite of Simon's six grandchildren.

"It's okay," said Simon. "I'm ready. I've lived a long and fruitful life. I'm not afraid to die. But I am concerned about how I might die. Just make sure I am dead before they put me in the ground."

Kenny cocked his head in bewilderment. "I don't think I heard you right, Grandpa."

Simon held out his calloused hand and clamped it hard against his grandson's wrist. "Kenny, promise me that when they close the coffin on me, I will be absolutely, positively dead."

"I promise, Grandpa," replied Kenny, wincing at the morbid thought. He looked lovingly at his grandfather and leaned over and kissed him. *He isn't making any sense,* Kenny thought. *Maybe his mind is getting feeble.*

"I know what you're thinking, Kenny. You think I'm going crazy, right?"

Kenny stood up, startled at how right his grandfather was. "Uh, no, of course not, Grandpa. Why, you have the sharpest mind in all of Montana."

"Kenny, pull up a chair. Let me tell you a painful secret I've harbored for over 70 years. It will explain my one and only fear in life—being buried alive."

Simon Bolt grew up in Missoula, Montana, a center for the logging industry. In 1920, when Simon was a strapping 15-year-old, he worked part-time with the lumberjacks, learning to wield an ax and use the two-man saw. His best friend, Rocky Livingston, was a year older and also part of the logging crew. The two were as close as brothers. They thought alike, talked alike, and even looked alike—both were tall and muscular and sported shaggy blond hair.

They worked hard and played even harder. In their free

time they loved to compete against each other—wrestling, swimming races, running the quarter mile. It didn't matter. They competed fiercely and fairly. And when the contest was over, they'd go off shaking hands while slinging good-natured jabs at each other. The winner owned the bragging rights over the other—until the next challenge.

During the summer, Simon and Rocky lived in a logging camp with their fathers, who were ace lumberjacks known as *fallers*, the men who chopped down the trees. The two teens were *buckers*, the workers who cut the fallen trunks into shorter lengths so the wood could be hauled out of the forest more easily. As buckers, Simon and Rocky used axes to lop off the limbs. Then they teamed up on the two-man crosscut saw—or "misery whip"—and sawed the trunks into smaller logs of 12 to 40 feet (3.5 m to 12 m) long.

It was backbreaking work, but the boys didn't mind. They were living in the great outdoors where forests of Douglas fir, ponderosa, and western larch echoed with the warning cry of "timber!"

Late in the summer, the boys trained for the annual loggers' competition, which featured games involving traditional lumberjack skills. Among the contests were ax throwing, log tossing, stump chopping, and log rolling.

Simon and Rocky practiced tossing a short-handled, double-headed ax at a target 20 feet (6 m) away. The target was a two-foot- (60-cm-) thick cross section of a log mounted on a stand and painted with a bull's-eye. Rocky usually bested Simon in this contest.

For another event the boys practiced splitting a foot- (30-cm-) thick, three-foot- (1-m-) long log into pieces small enough to fit into a three-inch (7.5-cm) hole. Simon was a faster chopper than Rocky.

Their fiercest rivalry involved log rolling, or as the loggers called it, burling. In this contest two competitors stood near opposite ends on an eight-foot- (2.5-m-) long log floating in the pond of the sawmill. Then by moving their feet forward or backward to get the log rolling, each tried to make the other guy lose his balance and fall into the water. The winner had to remain standing on the log.

It was a contest that required incredible balance and skill—and strategy. Every afternoon after work Rocky and Simon ran over to the sawmill pond and trained for the burling event. They were so evenly matched that they kept pitching each other into the drink.

A week before the annual loggers' competition, the boys were practicing hard. "This year, when it comes to burling, you're going for a swim," declared Simon.

"Forget it, pal," countered Rocky. "If anyone is going for a dive, it's you. This is my event. I own it."

"Not a chance. A quarter says I dump you on our first roll today."

"You're on!"

They stripped off their shirts and waded out in the shallow pond to a floating log. Carefully they hopped up on the log, stood up, and with their arms flapping to keep their balance, yelled, "Ready? Set! Go!"

Simon started spinning the log backward. Rocky countered by speeding up the rolling log and then tried to stop the spin by reversing the motion of his feet.

"Whoa, you almost got me," laughed Simon, barely able to

keep his balance. Hunched over with their arms spread out, both teens kept their eyes focused on their feet as they spun the log for 20 seconds, then 30 seconds—a personal best.

They started laughing, but their determination and competitiveness wouldn't allow either to give in for even a second. Twice, Simon nearly toppled into the water, but he kept pedaling stride for stride with Rocky. Finally Simon slowed the spinning log and then sped up, slowed down, and went in reverse as fast as he could. Rocky lurched forward and threw his arms back as a counterbalance. Simon zeroed in for the kill, and with one more quick spin with his feet, he had the log going so fast that Rocky couldn't keep up. Rocky's feet flew out from under him and he fell back headfirst with such force it looked like a perfect back dive off the side of a swimming pool.

"I'm the burling champ!" Simon shouted victoriously. "I win! I win! You owe me a quarter." He slowed the spinning log to a stop and waited for Rocky to surface. "C'mon, Rocky, you can't stay down there forever. C'mon back up and take your medicine like a man. Let me gloat."

When Rocky still didn't resurface, Simon figured that his best friend had swum away underwater so he wouldn't have to face any good-natured ribbing. Simon began to worry as he scanned the mill pond for nearly a minute without any sign of Rocky. No bubbles, no ripples.

"Okay, Rocky, the fun is over. C'mon up." Simon was getting more concerned with each passing second. "Hey, Rocky, this isn't funny. Where are you?"

The rays from the late afternoon sun bounced off the water, making it almost impossible to see into the pond.

Now fearing for his friend's safety, Simon leaped into the cold water at the spot where Rocky had fallen. Almost immediately he came across a patch of thick reeds before his hand hit something hard enough to scrape his knuckles. *Ouch, that hurt!* he thought. Hidden among the reeds stood a jagged rock in the shallow bottom. *Oh, no, I hope Rocky didn't hit his head on this rock,* he told himself. Frantically Simon looked around but couldn't find his friend. Running out of air, he returned to the surface, took a deep breath, and shouted, "Rocky! Where are you?"

Simon dived back down into the patch of reeds. Moments later his heart sank. He bumped into a work boot—and it was connected to a limp body entangled in the reeds. *It's Rocky! He's unconscious!* Simon clutched his friend's feet and freed him from the reeds. With his lungs about to burst, Simon grabbed Rocky from under his arms and pulled him to the surface. Simon then dragged him to the edge of the pond, where he saw that his best buddy had injured the back of his head.

"Help! Help!" Simon yelled. As workers from the sawmill rushed over, Simon slapped Rocky in the face, "Rocky, wake up! Wake up! He's not breathing." Simon and another worker tried desperately to revive Rocky, but he failed to respond. By the time the logging-camp physician, Doc Butterworth, arrived, it was too late.

The doctor draped his arm around Simon and said, "I'm afraid Rocky is dead. I can't detect a pulse. He probably drowned after he hit his head on the rock and was knocked out."

Doc Butterworth's words pierced Simon's heart like a

dagger. "No, he can't be dead!" cried Simon. "He just can't!" He threw himself across Rocky's prone body.

Doc Butterworth gently pried the shaken teen off the body. "I know it's a shock," he said. "I tried everything, but I have to pronounce him dead at"—he pulled out his pocket watch—"four twenty-two P.M."

Simon's mind swirled in a fog of grief. *Rocky, dead? This can't be happening! How could a little fall off a log cost Rocky his life?* He wanted to run away from this horrible scene, to wipe it from his mind. So Simon fled from the sawmill and into the woods, racing blindly through prickly bushes, thick underbrush, and muddy streams. He didn't care where he was going, only that he wanted to escape from the shocking accident. Simon ran until he collapsed deep in the woods.

Alone on his knees on the moss-covered ground, Simon wept until he had no tears left to shed. Then he sat down on a log and called up memories of his best friend: joyriding in a Model T Ford, fixing Mrs. Wilson's window after accidentally breaking it while playing baseball, sitting by the mill pond and talking about everything from girls, to the war, to death.

Simon remembered one particular day when Rocky's older brother Samuel joined them for a discussion about the afterlife. Samuel, a medical school student, told them he had once seen a ghost of a lumberjack who had been killed in a logging accident.

After listening to Samuel's account, Simon and Rocky said they believed in the possibility that a person could return from death as a spirit. Later, the two teens made a pact that whoever died first would try to contact the other one.

As he sat on the log alone in the woods, Simon glanced up, cleared his throat, and said out loud, "Rocky, if you're out there, please make yourself known. Tell me you're okay."

Simon looked around, waiting for some sign, any sign, to prove the existence of Rocky's ghost. He leaped up from his log when the stillness of the forest was shattered by the shrill call of a hawk circling above.

Two days after the fatal accident, Simon attended Rocky's funeral. Immediately after the services at the funeral home, the family was about to close the casket for the last time when Simon pleaded, "Please, not yet. Let me have a moment with him." Leaning over the coffin, Simon gazed down and touched his friend's hand. In his mind Simon told Rocky, *You feel so cold. And I feel so empty. This is supposed to be the final good-bye, but why do I keep thinking I'll see you again soon?* Simon stared long and hard at the body, hopelessly wishing that by some miracle Rocky would wake up. *Do something, Rocky. Wrinkle your nose, blink an eyelid, twitch a finger. Tell me you're not dead.*

Finally Rocky's father came over and put a hand on Simon's shoulder. "Son, it's time to close the casket."

Long after everyone left the cemetery, Simon remained near his friend's final resting place. He sat on the ground, leaned against a tombstone opposite Rocky's freshly covered grave, and chewed on a blade of grass. He wondered how long it would take for the ache in his heart to ease.

Suddenly an awesome pang of fear jolted Simon. It was a feeling that bordered on panic, as if he were losing a powerful struggle between life and death. The blood pulsed through his veins with so much speed that he thought his head was going to explode. Alarmed at this unexpected feeling of terror, Simon leaped to his feet, scanning the cemetery for the cause of this overwhelming fear. But there was no apparent explanation. Emotionally and physically exhausted, he sat on the ground, leaned against a tree opposite the grave, and fell fast asleep.

About a half hour after the sun set, Simon woke up with a start. He looked up and gasped. "Rocky! Is that really you?" Simon rubbed his eyes to make sure he wasn't dreaming. Standing in the dimming light next to the tombstone was Rocky, looking just as he did when Simon last saw him alive—shirtless and in jeans and work boots.

Simon was so shocked that he didn't know what to say. He simply shook his head in awe and broke out into a huge smile.

But the phantom didn't smile back. Instead, Rocky looked crushed and bewildered. In a voice weary with despair, he said, "Simon, I wasn't ready to die."

"I tried to save you, Rocky. I dived in the water and searched for you. When I found you, I freed you from the reeds, dragged you out, and tried to revive you. But it was too late."

"I wasn't ready to die," the ghost repeated. And then he slowly faded away.

"Rocky! Wait! Don't go!" After Rocky disappeared, Simon sat motionless, thunderstruck. *We always said the first one to die would contact the other one. And Rocky showed up. But did it really happen? Or am I so upset by Rocky's death that my mind is playing tricks on me? Geez, I'm so hurt by Rocky's death that now I'm imagining things. I don't dare tell anyone. They'll think I'm nuts.*

The following evening Simon returned to the graveyard. The spirit of his best buddy appeared once more. "I wasn't ready to die," said Rocky.

"I know," Simon replied. "No one ever is."

"You don't understand. Simon, they buried me when I wasn't even dead!"

"Not dead?"

"I was alive!"

"But how can that be? You had no heartbeat. You weren't breathing. You were turning blue. Doc Butterworth examined you and said you were dead. I felt you just before they closed the lid on your casket. You were cold and lifeless."

"I was alive," Rocky declared again. "Open my coffin and you will see what I mean." Then he vanished.

Rocky's chilling words left Simon in a state of shock. *If this really was Rocky's ghost, then he died the most horrible death imaginable!* Suddenly it dawned on Simon why he experienced that unexplained terror while sitting by Rocky's grave. *I was feeling Rocky's horror when he regained consciousness after he was buried and tried to escape from his grave! I was only a few feet above him. I could have saved him if only I had known!*

Or am I cracking up? I've got to find out for myself. But how? I can't do this by myself.

The next day Simon approached Rocky's older brother Sam and told him about the ghostly graveyard visits of the previous two nights.

"Sam, you must believe me. Rocky told me he was buried alive. I'll never rest until I know the truth."

"There's only one way to find out," said Sam. "But do you realize what you're asking?"

"Yes, I need your help to dig up Rocky's coffin. Look, no one has to know except you and me. We can do it tonight."

"What if we're caught?" asked Sam.

"People will assume we're crazy with grief. Nothing will happen to us."

"What if you're wrong about Rocky?"

"Then I really am crazy," Simon said grimly.

"And if you're right?"

"Then I will be heartbroken beyond belief."

Late that night Simon and Sam, armed with shovels, sneaked over to the cemetery. They worked swiftly and silently to remove the dirt from the grave until they reached the coffin.

"Are you sure you want to go through with this?" Sam asked.

"We've got to know," Simon replied.

Sam used his shovel to pry loose the top of the coffin. All they had to do now was open the lid. Simon took a deep breath. With one trembling hand holding a lantern, he slowly lifted the top.

Simon peered down inside, took a quick glance, and then cried out, "He was buried alive!"

Sam grabbed the lantern and looked for himself. Rocky's body was lying on its side, with his face in pain.

Sam was so choked up he could barely talk. "He tried to get out. Oh, how he must have suffered in his final minutes."

After Simon and Sam held each other and cried, Sam said, "I think I know what happened. When Rocky fell into the water and hit his head, he must have entered a state of catalepsy—a condition in which the victim appears to be dead but really isn't. I heard about this in medical school. His muscles became rigid, his breathing was so shallow it couldn't be detected, and his heartbeat couldn't be felt or heard. Doc Butterworth became convinced he was dead. But Rocky was still alive when they put him in the coffin. He probably woke up right after he was buried, realized where he was, and then tried to get out. He had no chance. He was doomed and he suffocated."

"I can't think of a worse way to die," shuddered Simon.

More than 70 years later the memories of his best friend's death and ghostly visit remained as vivid as ever for Simon Bolt.

"Kenny, now do you understand why I have this fear of being buried alive?" Simon asked his grandson.

"Yes. What a horrible way to die."

"And what a terrible secret I've had to carry all these years." Simon took another few breaths from his oxygen mask and added, "I didn't mean to scare you or burden you with this incident, but my fear is so strong I had to tell you. I trust you won't let what happened to Rocky happen to me."

"I give you my word, Grandpa."

Two weeks later Kenny, who lived in a town 20 miles (32 km) away from his grandfather, was walking home from the library when an elderly man approached him.

"Pardon me, son," said the old man, tipping his hat, a weathered baseball cap. "But I have a message for you."

Although Kenny had never seen the man before, he

noticed something oddly familiar about him. His kind, pale blue eyes tinged with hazel looked exactly like those of his grandfather's. "The message is from your grandpa. He said you don't have to worry about his secret anymore. His fear was unfounded. And, oh, yes, he said to look after Grandma and that he loves you very much."

The old man then tipped his hat again and walked on. Kenny stood stunned for a few seconds and then turned around to talk to the stranger. But he was nowhere in sight.

Kenny started to shake. *Who was that man? How could he disappear like that? And what did he mean by that message?*

Kenny learned the answer to the last question as soon as he returned home. When he stepped inside, he saw his mother sitting in a chair, crying.

"Mom, what's wrong?"

"Grandpa died about an hour ago," she replied. "His lungs and heart simply stopped working. He's at peace now."

Kenny was about to demand further medical proof that his grandfather was dead. But then Kenny thought about the encounter with the stranger minutes earlier and realized that somehow his grandfather had sent a message to comfort him. "Yes, Grandpa is at peace," said Kenny. "And he no longer has anything to fear."

THE SPIRIT OF THE WAVERLY INN

"Oh, dear," said Mrs. Calloway, owner of the Waverly Inn. "We seem to have a problem."

"We made our reservations two months ago for the two-bedroom suite," said Hugh Pulaski, his arms around his wife, Margie, and their nine-year-old daughter, Kristen.

"Yes, I know," replied Mrs. Calloway from behind her desk. "I remember taking it. But I thought you said your daughter was *nineteen,* not nine."

"So?"

"I'm afraid we don't allow children to stay at our bed-and-breakfast inn because our guests demand peace and quiet. We have only five bedrooms, so it's pretty intimate here. And you know how some kids can be—rowdy and disruptive."

Kristen glanced toward the hallway and spotted a girl about her age in a pink party dress that flared at the waist. The girl was leaning against the wall, staring directly at her. "What about her?" Kristen innocently asked the innkeeper, pointing to the girl.

The Pulaskis and Mrs. Calloway looked toward the hall, but it was empty.

"Who are you talking about?" asked Mrs. Calloway.

"I saw a girl standing there," Kristen replied.

"I can assure you that no child is here or ever has been here," Mrs. Calloway said huffily. "You must be mistaken."

"Look, ma'am," said Mr. Pulaski, "the fall colors are at their peak. We drove all the way from Washington, D.C., to spend the next four days enjoying the Vermont scenery. There isn't another room available around here for miles."

Mrs. Calloway gazed at Kristen and sighed. "Perhaps we can make an exception. I hope the other guests won't mind. Your room is on the first floor, last door on your right."

Once inside their suite Kristen walked through her parents' bedroom and into her room. "Oh, it's cute," she said, beaming. "Look, Mom, the bed has a canopy over it and a big thick comforter."

"It's darling," replied her mother. "Now, Kristen, you'll have to be on especially good behavior here, okay? But then, you usually are."

"I'll be good, but I don't care much for Mrs. Calloway."

Frost coated the windows by the time Kristen climbed into bed that night. Her room was drafty and chilly, so she snuggled under the blanket and pulled the comforter up to her neck.

During the night, she woke up and found herself curled in a ball, shivering from the cold. All the covers had fallen onto the floor. *I must have kicked them off while I was sleeping*, Kristen thought. She gathered up the blanket and comforter, spread them over her bed, slipped underneath them, and returned to her slumber.

An hour later Kristen awoke chilled to the bone with the covers piled on the floor again. She picked them up and got comfy again, but couldn't get back to sleep right away. So she began thinking about the drive she and her parents would take through the Green Mountains in the morning. But then her covers seemed to slip a bit. Kristen pulled them tighter around her neck. A minute later she felt gentle tugs on the covers as they inched down toward the foot of the bed.

Kristen slid out from under the covers and crawled to the end of the bed. In the darkness she leaned over and groped around where the comforter and blanket had bunched together. Her hand explored along the folds of the covers when suddenly she felt something ice cold. Cringing with alarm, Kristen tried to figure out what she was touching. *It feels like . . . FINGERS!*

Kristen let out a bloodcurdling scream. Then she leaped off the bed, bolted into the next room, and hopped onto her parents' bed.

"Kristen, what's the matter?" asked her mother.

"Someone is in my room, pulling down my bed covers!"

Her father dashed into her room, flipped on the light, and looked around. Other than the covers piled up on the floor at the foot of the bed, nothing looked out of place. He searched under the bed and in the closet. "Honey, everything looks all right," he announced. "There's no one in your room."

"But I felt someone's fingers pulling my covers at the foot

49

of my bed," Kristen claimed. "Really I did."

Just then Mrs. Calloway knocked on their door. "Is everything all right?"

"Yes," replied Mrs. Pulaski. "Kristen just had a nightmare. I'm sorry if she disturbed you."

"Oh, I see," the owner said with slight irritation in her voice. "I hope she'll be able to go back to sleep. I hope we *all* can. Good night."

"Mommy," said Kristen. "It wasn't a nightmare."

"Honey, there's only one door to your room, and it connects to our room. The window is shut tight. There's no way somebody could have entered your room. You had a very realistic dream, that's all."

"Okay," said Kristen, still full of doubts.

"Want to sleep with us tonight?"

"Yes."

When Kristen woke up the next morning, she noticed her parents had left her a note on the pillow: "Kristen, we let you sleep late. We're having breakfast in the dining room."

Kristen dressed and walked out into the hallway. About 40 feet (12 m) away, where the hall meets the parlor, she spotted the same girl from the day before. The girl, about Kristen's age, had short straight brown hair with bangs in the front. She was wearing the same pink party dress and had white anklets and black shoes. Her skin was pale and her face expressionless.

"Hi," said Kristen.

The girl nodded, smiled, and then walked into the parlor.

"Wait!" Kristen called out. "I want to talk to you."

Kristen hustled into the parlor, but the only person there

was a guest, Dr. Felix Savant. The bearded bushy-haired professor was writing a postcard.

"Excuse me," said Kristen. "Where did that girl go?"

"No one has been in here since I sat down about ten minutes ago," he replied.

Perplexed, Kristen joined her parents in the dining room where several guests were eating breakfast. Her parents introduced her to the others at the table, including the Whartons, an elderly couple.

"I'm sorry if I woke up anybody last night," Kristen said. "I guess I had a nightmare."

They all assured her it was all right. "It's kind of a novelty having a little girl stay here," said Mrs. Wharton. "My husband and I have been coming to the inn for the past eight years, and I've never known a child to be a guest."

Mrs. Calloway walked into the room with a basket of hot rolls. "That's right, Kristen, you're the first—and only."

"But I just saw a girl in the hallway, the same one I saw yesterday."

"That's impossible, dear," the innkeeper said. "As I told you before, there is no other child here."

"She was wearing a pink party dress."

"My, you have a vivid imagination."

After breakfast Kristen went back to her room to get her coat for the day's outing. Only then did she notice a cane, a pair of glasses, and a scarf lying on her bed. They weren't hers or her parents. She picked them up and was carrying them down the hallway when she heard several guests complaining to Mrs. Calloway. Mr. Wharton couldn't find his cane, Mrs. Bittner was missing her favorite scarf, and another guest, Mr. Cochrane, was searching for his glasses.

A flustered Mrs. Calloway kept shaking her head. "Why would anyone take your things?" When she saw Kristen carrying the different items, the owner declared, "Aha! There's your answer."

"I found them in my room on my bed," said Kristen. "I don't know how they got there."

She didn't like the way Mrs. Calloway raised her eyebrows and glared at her.

That night Kristen decided to sleep in her bedroom rather than stay with her parents. "I'm a big girl, Daddy. I can sleep alone. Just do me one favor, please. Tuck in the blanket and comforter so they won't fall off."

Her dad secured the covers and said, "There, it's just like a cocoon. Good night, sweetheart. Sleep tight."

Unfortunately, Kristen didn't. Just as she was falling asleep, she felt an itch on her ear and scratched it. Then her feet began to tickle. She jerked her knees up to her chin and scratched her feet. After stretching her legs, Kristen felt a tickling sensation on her forehead as if someone had touched her face with a feather. "Stop it, Mommy," she said.

Kristen sat up in her bed. *It can't be Mom. I'm alone. Something must be in my bed!* She ripped off the covers and turned on the light. She shook the sheets and the blanket.

Then Kristen heard a strange giggle followed by a child's voice softly singing, "This old man, he played one. He played knick-knack on my thumb . . . This old man, he played two. He played knick-knack on my shoe." Kristen searched around her room, trying to find the girl. "This old man, he played three, he played knick-knack on my knee . . ."

Several loud raps on the wall caused Kristen to jump.

"Please quit singing! It's one o'clock in the morning!" It was Mrs. Wharton, shouting from the room on the other side of the wall.

"It's not me!" Kristen yelled back. She was about to run into her parents' room when she saw the little girl in the pink dress standing in the corner.

"Who are you?" a startled Kristen asked.

"Amanda," she replied with a curtsy. "I like that song, don't you? My mommy would sing it to me lots of times."

"What are you doing in my room?"

"I thought we could play."

"At one in the morning?"

Amanda shrugged.

"Are you the one who pulled the covers off me last night and tickled me tonight?" Kristen asked.

Amanda smiled and giggled. "Yes."

"Where are you from?"

"The Waverly Inn."

"But Mrs. Calloway said—"

"What does she know?" said Amanda, flicking her hand.

"How did you get in here?"

"No more questions. Play with me."

"It's late," said Kristen. "I think you'd better leave."

"I can't. I'm stuck here." Amanda's lips began to quiver, and tears trickled down her face. She put her head in her hands and began to sob.

"Please, don't cry," said Kristen. "You're going to wake

everybody up."

Just then her parents barged into the room. "Kristen, are you okay?" asked her father. "Why are you crying?"

"I'm not crying. She is." Kristen pointed to Amanda. But she had vanished.

"Who are you talking about?" asked her mother.

"Amanda. The girl I've seen the last two days. She showed up tonight in my room. Except she's not here now."

"Dreaming again?"

"No, I wasn't! This girl was definitely in my room."

Mrs. Calloway knocked on the door. "Is everything okay?"

"Sorry, Mrs. Calloway," Mrs. Pulaski replied. "Kristen had another nightmare."

"I see," she replied coldly. "Well, I hope for her sake—and everyone else's—that she sleeps through the rest of the night."

Kristen grabbed her mother's hand. "Mommy, I really hate it here. Can we leave in the morning? Please?"

"We might as well. I have a feeling we're going to get thrown out of here anyway."

Kristen climbed into bed with her mother while her father slept in the other room. Nothing happened the rest of the night. About 8 A.M., after her parents had gone to breakfast, Kristen woke up in confusion and fear. Someone was pinching her hard on the thigh, arm, and neck. She rose up in bed, but two icy hands clamped around her face and shoved her back down. The attacker's hands covered her mouth and muffled her screams.

As Kristen squirmed and struggled, panic surged through her body. *Who's doing this? I can't breathe! I've got to get free!*

With every ounce of strength left in her body, Kristen thrashed on her bed until she tumbled to the floor.

"Be quiet and I'll let you go," whispered her attacker. Kristen recognized the voice. It was Amanda's! "Promise not to run or scream, okay?"

Kristen quit fighting and nodded. Amanda released her grip, and Kristen spun around on the floor to face her. "Why were you pinching me?" Kristen demanded.

"I'm mad at you because you want to leave."

"You can't blame me. I mean, you've scared me, hurt me, and gotten me into trouble. Mrs. Calloway hates me."

Amanda pouted and cast her eyes down. "I'm lonely. I want to be with my mommy. Will you help me find her?"

"If I can. When did you last see her?"

"Right before I died."

Kristen's eyes grew wide. "You're talking scary. I'm getting out of here." Kristen rose to her feet and hurriedly dressed into jeans and a sweatshirt.

"Don't leave!" demanded Amanda. "Or you'll be sorry!"

As Kristen reached for the doorknob, she heard a loud thud. She turned around and was stunned to see the foot of the bed raise by itself before slamming to the floor. Then the head of the bed rose and fell down. CRASH! Next, the bedside lamp smashed to the floor into dozens of pieces.

Kristen screamed and tore out of the room and into the hall where her parents and several guests were rushing toward her. "I didn't do it!" Kristen cried. "I swear I didn't do it! It was Amanda!"

"Who's Amanda?" asked her mother.

"The girl who lives here!"

"No girl lives here," declared Mrs. Calloway.

"Well, then it's the girl who died here!" Kristen threw her hands up in the air and shook her head in despair. "Oh, I don't know what's going on. Amanda told me she lived here and was looking for her mother. And I know this sounds crazy, but Amanda told me she hasn't seen her mother since *Amanda herself died*!"

"Why, that's absurd," said Mrs. Calloway. Looking sternly at the Pulaskis, she added, "I do hope you get your daughter some help."

"Pardon me, folks," said Dr. Savant. "Forgive me for butting in, but I often investigate paranormal incidents—happenings that cannot easily be explained. Let me talk to Kristen alone, if I may."

After Kristen had calmed down, the two went into the parlor, where she recalled in detail her encounters with Amanda. "Kristen, I believe you," he told her. "It's very possible Amanda is a ghost."

Kristen's jaw dropped open, and a chill slithered up her spine. "I'll never sleep alone the rest of my life."

"Sure you will," Dr. Savant said reassuringly, "once we solve this case." He and Kristen joined the other guests in the dining room. "Mrs. Calloway," he asked. "Are you aware of any unexplained sights or sounds in this inn?"

"None at all, and I've owned the inn for ten years," she replied. "There are no ghosts here, if that's what you mean."

"I believe there is one," he said. "I felt its presence yesterday morning in the parlor and later in the hallway. I think the spirit of this ghost materialized in the presence of the first child ever to stay at the inn. Mrs. Calloway, do you know anything about the history of this place? Maybe a child died here before you bought it."

"Come to think of it, the previous owner, Stella Lynch, had a young daughter who mysteriously disappeared," said the innkeeper. "Talk about tragedy upon tragedy. Days after the girl was reported missing, Mrs. Lynch was killed in a car accident. They never found out what happened to the girl. Some people said Mrs. Lynch was nuts and murdered her."

"Amanda could be buried somewhere in this house," said Dr. Savant. "Based on what she told Kristen, I believe her spirit won't rest until her body can lay next to her mother's, whom I assume was buried in a cemetery."

"A body in my inn?" exclaimed Mrs. Calloway, pressing her hand against her chest. "No offense, Dr. Savant, but I find this hard to swallow. However, for the sake of argument, if there really is a ghost of a child here, what do we do?"

Kristen, her parents, Mrs. Calloway, and Dr. Savant sat around a table in the parlor with the curtains drawn to conduct a seance. "Chances are Amanda won't appear to us as she did to Kristen, but she might still communicate with us," said the professor.

After lighting a candle, they held hands and let Dr. Savant start the seance. "Amanda, we want to help you find your mother," said the professor. "But you have to help us. Tell us where your body is buried."

Suddenly a loud knock came from the other side of the room. The professor walked over and put his hand on the wall. "Amanda, is your body behind this wall?"

They heard several new thumps from another part of the

house. "It's coming from the kitchen," said Mrs. Calloway.

They hurried into the kitchen. "Lead me to you, Amanda," said Dr. Savant. The rapping sound then moved down the hall to the Whartons' room. A minute later they heard knocking coming from the Pulaskis' suite. And then it moved into Kristen's room in the wall behind a huge oak dresser.

The rapping grew so loud the room shook and then it fell silent. They waited for more knocking but none came.

"Is this the spot, Amanda?" asked Dr. Savant.

The professor moved the dresser out of the way. "Look at that," said Kristen's dad. "It's obvious there once was a closet here that had been plastered over."

"Mrs. Calloway, do we have your permission to break through the wall?" asked the professor.

"Anything to put an end to this frightening ordeal," she said. "There are tools in the basement."

Moments later Dr. Savant and Mr. Pulaski used a sledgehammer and an ax to break through the wall. When the plaster fell away and the dust settled, everyone gasped. The hole in the wall revealed a small white coffin.

Kristen began shaking. "I don't want to look," she said tearfully, burying her head in her mother's stomach.

"We'll wait for the authorities to open it," the professor announced.

Mr. Pulaski noticed a yellowed envelope lying on the floor of the closet and picked it up. "It's a letter. It says, 'To Whom It May Concern: Here lies my daughter, Amanda Lynch. She was the sweetest girl in the world—the light of my life. I loved her with every ounce of my being. But she was cruelly snatched from me by an illness that happened so swiftly she died before I could get her to a doctor. I couldn't bear to part with her. I wanted her to be with me always. So I kept her here. If I have broken any laws, forgive me. I acted solely out of a love that will never die for Amanda.' It's signed Stella Lynch."

Dr. Savant kneeled in front of Kristen and asked, "Are you all right?" Kristen nodded, but not very convincingly.

"Apparently, when you arrived at the inn, Amanda's ghost felt it was safe to make herself known to you because you were about her age," explained the professor. "She desperately wanted your help. And through you, she was able to get that help."

When the authorities arrived, they opened the coffin and found the body of a young girl in a pink party dress. They later determined it was Amanda Lynch.

Amanda's ghost soon got her wish. She was buried in the same cemetery in a plot next to her mother, Stella.

The Waverly Inn was never bothered by a ghost again.

CONFESSION FROM THE BEYOND

Fifteen-year-old Travis Sheehan thought it would be fun to live in Artemus Simms's farmhouse for a week while the old man visited relatives.

For Travis, it turned out to be the most terrifying time of his life.

Staying alone in the old two-story frame house outside the town of Roseville began as an adventure. No curfew, no rules, no parents. It wasn't as nice as his home; the furniture belonged in a thrift shop. But the place had all the modern conveniences, even cable TV. And Mr. Simms was paying him for the work he'd be doing.

Travis, a strapping six-foot (183-cm), 175-pound (79-kg) athlete, wasn't afraid to be alone in the old house. But he didn't sleep too well the first night. That's because the bed was lumpy, and the house creaked and groaned in the wind.

As he tended to the farmer's few cows, pigs, and chickens, Travis felt sorry for the man. The son of a son of a farmer, Artemus Simms had worked the land his whole life. Nearing the age of 75, he had sold most of his acreage and owned only a small plot that he farmed.

Artemus Simms had a sadness about him. Old-timers said that back in his twenties his hair turned white almost overnight. No one knew why, but Simms changed from a caring, happy-go-lucky young man into a distant sad loner who seemed to carry the weight of the world on his shoulders. Whatever happened to him, neighbors said, must have been tragic.

During his first day alone at the farm, Travis had finished feeding the hogs when he leaned against the fence. The post suddenly snapped off at the base, sending him reeling into the mud with a big splat.

"What a mess!" Travis complained to himself as he tried to wipe the dripping mud off his clothes. Later, he examined the post and discovered it had rotted at the base. Travis went into the barn, got a shovel, and began digging a hole deep enough for a new post that he found.

As he dug, his shovel struck something hard and shiny. *What's that?* he wondered. He reached down and pulled out a gold object caked with mud. *It's a gold pocket watch! Wow!*

Travis cleaned the mud off the gold casing, opened it up, and was amazed to find that the crystal hadn't broken. The face of the watch was white with numbers in ornate Roman numerals. The long delicate minute hand and the shorter hour hand seemed in excellent shape. Carefully he wound the watch. To his surprise, it worked.

This is so cool. I wonder if Mr. Simms lost it. Travis studied the scratched and dented casing. On the back were engraved the initials RTS. *I guess it didn't belong to Artemus Simms.*

Maybe it was a relative's. I'll keep it in the house and tell him about it when he comes back. Travis finished installing the post and repaired the fence to the pigpen.

That night he was almost asleep when he heard someone running from the barn. The pigs were snorting and cows were mooing. Travis peered out the window and didn't see anyone, but he went outside to investigate.

As he calmed the animals, Travis had the feeling he was being watched. Suddenly he caught a glimpse of someone dashing behind the toolshed. Travis ran after him, but quickly lost sight of the trespasser.

He walked back into the house and locked the door. When he returned to his bedroom, he noticed that the old pocket watch was lying on the floor. *That's strange,* he thought. *I left it on the dresser. I wonder how it fell.*

He climbed back into bed and closed his eyes. Suddenly he was jarred by BANG, BANG, BANG. The old shutters on the upstairs windows began violently slamming against the house. Travis bolted out of bed and looked outside. *Why are they banging like that? There's no wind. Everything else looks quiet out there.* Then, as fast as they started, the shutters stopped their battering.

Before Travis could make sense of the incident, he caught sight of a figure skulking by the house. In the moonlight it looked like a man in a floppy wide-brim hat, light shirt, dark pants, and boots. Travis blinked and tried to focus his eyes, but when he looked again, the person was gone.

So somebody is outside. He doesn't look like any of my friends. A burglar maybe? His heart began to speed up. Travis hurried into the kitchen and grabbed a knife for protection. As he checked to make sure all the doors and windows were locked, he didn't feel quite as safe as he had before. *Why did I take this job? Maybe I should sleep at home at night. But if I do that, then everybody will think I'm chicken. No, I can't do that.*

When Travis returned to his bedroom, he locked the door behind him and then felt sick to his stomach. The pocket watch now was on the end table. *I put it back on the dresser. I know I did. Didn't I? I'm so rattled, maybe I forgot I had left it on the table.*

As he fingered the watch, he again experienced a strong feeling that he was not alone. Suddenly he heard the creaking of the closet door slowly opening.

"Who's there?" he called out. "Be careful! I have a knife—and I'll use it."

Travis flicked on the light switch and then cautiously advanced toward the closet door, which had opened fully by itself. With his knife raised, Travis lunged inside. He found nothing but old clothes draped neatly on hangers.

The next night Travis stayed up as late as he could, watching television until he couldn't keep his eyes open any longer. When he sleepily returned to his room, he opened the door and gasped in startled surprise. Standing in the room, looking at the pocket watch, was the man he had seen prowling around the toolshed the night before.

The intruder, who had his back to Travis, slowly turned around, his head bowed and his floppy hat concealing his identity. As he lifted his head, the hallway light revealed a face so hideous Travis stumbled backward out of the room. The man's shriveled lips were twisted in a grimace, and his coal-black eyes were sunk so deep into his skull, it looked as if he had none.

His white shirt and brown pants were ripped. The fingers on his shaky hands were curled up and pasty white.

Travis screamed and bounded down the stairs in two leaps. He flew out the door and raced to the barn before he tumbled into a pile of hay. As he tried to catch his breath, his mind whirled in fear and awe. *What did I just see? Am I freaking out? Was it real? Was it a monster? A ghost? A figment of my imagination? Should I call the police? And tell them what? That there's a monster in the house? Right. I'll be the laughingstock of Roseville for sure.*

Wait a second. I'll bet it's one of my friends wearing a Halloween mask! Of course, that's what it is! But how did he get in the house? Hmmm, what if it isn't a joke? What if it's real? I won't know unless I go back inside.

With his heart beating wildly, Travis returned to the house. He grabbed a butcher knife from the kitchen drawer and fearfully walked up the stairs. His mouth dry and his armpits sweating, Travis kept hoping he would not come face to face with the monster; that it was all a joke pulled by one of his buddies.

"If this is Tony or Jeb or Rob, you're in big trouble!" Travis announced. "The game is over!"

What if it's not a joke? Be ready for anything, Travis.

Step by step Travis climbed the stairs, getting closer and closer to an unknown fate. When he reached the top landing, he stood still, waiting to hear a sound from the intruder. But all he heard was his own heavy breathing. He then headed toward the bedroom door. It was closed.

I know I didn't shut it when I ran down the stairs. So that means I didn't imagine him. He must be inside. If it's one of the guys, I'll get even by scaring him. But if it's not . . . He tried to swallow, but his mouth was too dry. *Okay, Travis, ready? One . . . two . . . three!* He flung the door open, leaped inside, and yelled at the top of his lungs.

Brandishing his knife and whipping around the room, he frantically looked for the intruder. But Travis was all alone. Nothing had been disturbed. His billfold was sitting on the dresser along with his keys. And the pocket watch was . . . *Hey, what's it doing on my bed?*

Travis snatched the watch and scampered back downstairs. He went into the living room and placed the knife and watch on the coffee table. He sat on the couch, wrapped himself up in a quilt, and tried to sort out the details of his terrifying night. Nothing made any sense.

For more than an hour he remained glued to the couch until his brain grew weary from thinking and worrying. And then he heard footsteps advancing toward the house from outside. They thumped onto the porch. He got up, grabbed the knife, and leaned beside the front door, ready to pounce on the stranger. He heard the click of the lock and saw the door swing open.

Travis jumped out into the doorway and screamed, "Ahhh!"

"Ahhh!" came the reply. The person at the door was so startled that he almost tumbled off the porch.

"Oh, my gosh!" stammered Travis. "Mr. Simms! I'm so sorry. I didn't know it was you!" Travis tossed the knife aside. He reached down and helped the farmer to his feet.

"Well, who else did you expect to come into the house?" grumbled Mr. Simms.

"I wasn't expecting you for another two days."

"Well, I saw all I wanted of my sisters, so I drove on home. My, you gave me a fright."

"I'm so sorry, sir. It was getting a little spooky around here, and I guess I was being extra cautious."

"Perhaps I should have called," said Mr. Simms, patting Travis on the back. "No real harm done. Everything go okay?"

Travis wanted to tell about the scary intruder. But before he could say anything, Mr. Simms's face curled into shock. "Where did you get this!" he demanded angrily, pointing to the pocket watch. The farmer gingerly picked it up as his fingers began to tremble. He turned the watch over and over in his big hands and snapped, "Answer me!"

"I found it next to the pigsty. A fence post broke, so I decided to put in a new one. I found the watch while I was digging the hole."

"Do you know what you've done?" demanded Mr. Simms.

"All I did was find a pocket watch in the mud. I thought you'd be pleased."

"Well, I'm not!"

"I don't understand, sir."

Mr. Simms angrily waved his hand in disgust. He continued to stare at the watch, mumbling to himself and shaking his head. Travis couldn't tell if he was angry or upset. Mr. Simms's whole body began to quiver, and he slumped into a chair.

"Sir, are you all right?"

"No," the old man replied weakly. "I feel dizzy. I think I need to lie down."

"Let me help you." Travis assisted Mr. Simms to his feet and gently led him upstairs and into the master bedroom. All the while the farmer clutched the watch and tears streamed down his face.

Travis knew that now wasn't a good time to talk about all the frightening occurrences in the house. Because it was so late, Travis decided to spend the night there and then call his parents for a ride home the next day.

As Travis sat up in bed, he wondered about the strange behavior of Mr. Simms. *Why did he react that way over the watch? I didn't do anything wrong. I found the watch and planned to give it to him. Why is he so angry with me? Man, I can't wait to get out of this place. Between him and all the scary things that have happened, I don't ever want to step foot in this house again.*

Travis glanced at the clock. It read 11:25. Moments later he was jolted by a loud thump coming from Mr. Simms's bedroom on the other side of the wall.

"Mr. Simms?" Travis shouted at the wall. "Is that you? Are you all right?" There was no answer.

Travis tossed and turned but couldn't get to sleep. So he picked up a book and read until the wee hours of the morning, when he again got the feeling that he was being watched. Slowly he lowered his book and peeked over it. Standing in the doorway of his bedroom was Mr. Simms.

"I know it's nearly three A.M., but I saw your light was on," said the farmer. "Travis, my boy, I owe you an apology for my behavior—and I owe you an explanation." He walked over to

67

a chair and sat down. The old man looked so different than he did earlier in the evening. The wrinkles appeared less severe, his eyes more peaceful, his voice very calm. His hands, still fondling the pocket watch, no longer trembled.

"This pocket watch belonged to my father, Remington Taylor Simms."

"That's what the initials RTS stand for on the back, right?" asked Travis.

"Yes. My father was a farmer and livestock dealer. Each year, in late fall, he and his hired hands drove a herd of cattle to market. It took them a week to get there. It wasn't easy, but they managed. The real danger took place on the return trip. It was common for armed robbers to lay in wait in the woods, ready to steal the money from livestock dealers returning from the sale of their cattle.

"Back then, the nearest bank was 20 miles (32 km) away, so my father kept his money at home in a secret place in the house. He and I took turns guarding the house with our guns for weeks after his return.

"One fall my father and his men set out on the long drive to market. I was twenty-two years old at the time, and I stayed behind to manage the farm and look after my mother and two younger sisters. About two days before my father was due home, I began staying up late at night to be on the lookout for any robbers who might try to ambush my father when he returned with his money.

"The first night—a windy, rainy dark night—I stood outside by the toolshed, waiting patiently for any sign of robbers. Shortly after midnight I saw someone move behind the bushes near the barn, so I sneaked up for a closer look. I saw a man prowling around the barn, and I yelled, 'Stop or I'll shoot!' The man kept walking. I decided to fire a warning shot, but I was so nervous that I aimed too low and shot him.

"I rushed over to him, but it was too dark to see anything. All I knew was that I had killed him. I panicked. I had never shot at anyone before in my life. I didn't know what to do. So I dragged the body to a far corner of the barn by the pigsty and covered it with mud.

"I didn't tell another breathing soul about what I had done. The next few nights I guarded our house for more possible robbers, but nothing happened. Then the hired hands arrived without my father. They said they had an argument with him over wages, so they left him.

"My family was quite concerned, because my father was so overdue. Then a vicious rumor started that he hadn't planned to come back; that he had run off with the money.

"Despite my worry about his whereabouts, I was racked with guilt over killing a would-be robber. I couldn't sleep at night, I had blinding headaches and stabbing pains in my stomach. I kept telling myself I was merely defending my home and family.

"Then the terror began. Night after night I was haunted by a ghost."

The hair on Travis's neck stood straight up. Breathlessly he asked Mr. Simms, "Was he wearing a floppy hat, white shirt, dark pants, and boots?"

"So you saw him too!" exclaimed Mr. Simms. "I'm not surprised."

"Who is he?"

"I'll tell you soon enough. First let me finish my story. The ghost was trying to tell me something, and I knew what I had to do even though I didn't want to do it. I forced myself to go to the pigsty. I dug up the body. There was no doubt it looked exactly like the ghost that had been haunting me.

"And then I saw a gold chain attached to his belt. I yanked on it—and pulled out the one object in this whole world that turned my life upside down forever. It was a pocket watch, this pocket watch"—his hands began to shake—"with the initials RTS on the back. I recognized it instantly. I covered my face with my hands and cried out, 'Oh, what have I done!' Travis, I had mistakenly killed my own father!"

Mr. Simms began to sob. As he wiped the tears with his sleeve, he continued. "I ripped the pocket watch off the chain and threw it in the pigsty. I was afraid to tell anyone of my horrible deed. So I secretly built a pine casket and buried my father in the family cemetery out on the hill overlooking the farmhouse. I marked his grave with three large stones in a triangle.

"I was never the same after that. My hair went from blond to white almost overnight."

Mr. Simms kept fondling the pocket watch. "I wanted to bury him with his watch. The day after I uncovered his body, I went looking for the watch, but I couldn't find it in all the mud. It remained in the muck all these years until you found it."

Travis then told Mr. Simms all the weird and frightening things that had happened while he was away. After he finished his story, Travis said, "Mr. Simms, all the strange things that happened to me began right after I found the watch. The unexplained noises, the banging shutters, and then seeing the ghost. It had to be the ghost of your father."

"The discovery of the watch must have stirred his spirit."

"He certainly stirred things up around here. Actually, he scared me to death."

"He is not at peace, Travis, and neither am I."

"But it was an accident," said Travis kindly. "He never would have been shot had he just told you who he was, or if you had recognized him."

"I know why it happened, Travis. About a year after his death, I learned that my father had suspected his own men were planning to rob him on the trip home. So he split from them. Because he was traveling alone, he wore a disguise—the floppy hat and other clothes—in case he met up with them on the way back.

"His horse pulled up lame a few miles from the house, so he walked the rest of the way. When he arrived at our farm late that night, he didn't hear my warning in the wind and rain. Or maybe he thought the men might be lying in wait for him. But as it turned out, it wasn't his men he had to fear." His voice cracked and he muttered, "It was his own son."

"Mr. Simms, why are you telling me this?"

"Because now is the right time—the only time."

Travis gazed out the window at the moonlit cemetery beyond the barn where Remington Simms was buried. The teen turned back to say something to Mr. Simms, but the old man was gone. He left behind the pocket watch on the chair where he had sat.

Travis never did get to sleep that night. At daybreak he finished his chores and went back into the house to say good-bye to Mr. Simms and to collect his money.

Although it was 10 A.M., he hadn't seen the old man yet

that morning. Travis went upstairs and peeked inside Mr. Simms's bedroom. "Sir, I'm ready to leave now. Mr. Simms? Are you up? Oh, no!"

The elderly farmer was sprawled on the floor, dead.

"It looks as if he died of a heart attack," said the coroner, after examining the body in the bedroom. He turned to the police and paramedics and said, "Time of death was probably eleven twenty-five P.M."

"No, it had to be closer to three A.M.," said Travis. "He was in my room talking to me."

"Son, I can tell he died much earlier," said the coroner. "Besides, when he started to fall, he hit the bedside table, knocked off the clock radio, and broke it. Look at the time on the clock—eleven twenty-five."

Travis snapped his fingers. "The thud! I heard a loud thump coming from his room at that time. It was probably Mr. Simms falling to the floor. But how could I have seen him more than three hours later?"

Only then did the shocking truth dawn on him. *It wasn't Mr. Simms I was talking to in my room last night. It was his ghost—and it confessed to me!*

After Travis revealed the tragic story to the Simms's family, they went to the cemetery and found the spot—three rocks forming a triangle—where Remington Simms had been buried. Soon after, they unearthed the skeleton of a middle-aged man.

Remington Simms and his son Artemus were eventually put in new coffins side by side on the hilltop graveyard—but not before the family granted Travis's wish and placed the pocket watch in Remington Simms's casket.

THE
GHOSTLY HOUSE CALL

For two days and two nights the screeching wind, vicious lightning, and pelting rain ravaged the Canadian province of New Brunswick. The ferocious storm hit one rural area in the northwest especially hard, knocking down trees and triggering floods.

Holed up in their quaint two-story house in the country, Gil and Lindy Dunlap were less concerned about the awful weather than they were about their extremely ill eight-year-old daughter, Marci. For the last 48 hours she had been suffering from a high fever, congestion in her lungs, breathing difficulties, and aches and pains.

As night fell, Lindy sat next to Marci's bed trying to comfort the little girl, who had broken out in a cold sweat and shivers. "Mommy," said Marci as she pulled the bedcovers tightly up to her neck, "I keep feeling worse. When will I get better?"

"Soon I hope," said Lindy. She bent over and gently brushed Marci's long, sweat-soaked brown hair off her flaming forehead. "Your fever keeps rising, and we're out of medicine," said Lindy. "How about drinking some more soda? You need liquids to help fight the fever."

"I don't want anything now," Marci moaned.

A flash of lightning followed instantly by a house-shaking KA-BOOM sent the lights in the house flickering.

"That was right outside my window, Mommy. I'm scared."

"I know. It's a bad storm, but we'll be all right. This house has been around for many years and seen its share of bad weather."

KA-BOOM . . . CRACK. A lightning bolt slammed into a maple tree in the front yard. A large branch split from the trunk and crashed to the ground.

Marci cringed. "Mommy, please stay with me."

"Okay, honey, move over." Lindy slipped into Marci's bed and held her tight, singing softly to her until the little girl fell asleep.

Lindy then got up and went downstairs, where Gil was listening to the latest weather report on the radio. "There's no letup in sight," Gil told her. "The storm is expected to last another two days. Authorities are warning people to stay off the roads. It's hazardous to drive because of downed trees and flooding. How's Marci?"

"She's asleep, but I'm getting worried," Lindy replied. "Her temperature is still climbing. It's 102 degrees."

"We really should get her to the doctor tomorrow if she's not any better."

Another too-close-for-comfort lightning strike and earth-shattering thunder jolted Marci awake. She was about to put her pillow over her head to drown out the storm when a bright flash briefly lit up her darkened room. It was then that she saw a man standing in the corner of the room.

"Daddy, is that you?" Marci asked.

All she heard in response was the howling wind, driving rain, and booming thunder. During another flash of lightning, Marci got a second quick look at the stranger. He was a tall gray-haired man in a long white coat.

"Who are you?" asked Marci.

Again there was no answer. She flicked on the light by her bed, but he was gone.

"Daddy! Mommy! Come quick!" Marci shouted.

Both parents raced upstairs. "What's wrong, angel?" asked Gil.

"There was a man in my room. He was standing right by my dresser!"

"Are you sure, honey?" asked Lindy.

"I'm positive! He was right over there!"

"Where did he go?" Gil asked.

"I don't know. When I turned on the light, he was gone."

Gil looked under the bed, searched the closet, and checked the window, which was locked. "There's no one here and no sign of anyone being here. The door to your room was closed when we heard you call us. Angel, I think you were dreaming or seeing things. A fever can do that to you."

"But he seemed so real," said Marci.

Lindy felt Marci's forehead and took her temperature again. "Your fever is rising. It's 102.8. Gil, we've got to get her some help."

"I'll call the doctor." He picked up the phone and slammed it down in frustration. "It's dead. The phone lines must be knocked out by the storm."

"Maybe we should take her to the emergency room at the hospital," said Lindy.

"It's fifteen miles (twenty-four km) from here." He glanced out the window. "The storm isn't getting any better. But we should try driving to the emergency room anyway."

They bundled up Marci and jumped into their pickup truck for the dangerous drive into town. In the blowing rain the truck chugged along on the slick road, dodging fallen limbs and other debris.

"Gil, look out!" screamed Lindy.

The beams of the headlights shined on a figure standing in the middle of the road only a few yards in front of them. An elderly man in a white knee-length coat waved his arms over his head, warning them to stop.

Gil slammed on the brakes, and the truck began skidding sideways on the rain-swept road before coming to a rest on the shoulder. "Is everyone all right?" asked Gil, once he stopped shaking.

"Yes, we're okay," replied Lindy. "Did you hit him?"

"I don't know. I didn't feel or hear a thud. Still, it would be a miracle if we missed him. He just appeared out of nowhere right in front of us. There was no way to avoid him."

Gil grabbed a flashlight, dashed out into the storm, and searched the road and both shoulders. When he returned to the truck, he told them, "I couldn't find the man anywhere, and there are no dents on the front of the truck that would indicate we struck him."

"That's so weird," said Lindy.

"Mommy, Daddy, that's the man I saw in my room tonight," said Marci.

"Are you absolutely sure?" asked Lindy.

"That was him."

"Marci, it must be the fever getting to you," said Gil. "There was no man in your room."

"Yes, there was—and it was him," Marci insisted. "He had gray hair and a long white coat."

"Gil, did you notice anything strange about him?" asked Lindy.

"He wasn't wearing any rain gear."

"Not only that, but he didn't even look wet," she said. "Here it is pouring like the dickens, and he looked absolutely dry as a bone."

Gil shook his head. "Who do you suppose he was?"

"I've never seen him before."

"He was obviously warning us about something."

"I wish we weren't out here," said Lindy. "This storm is just awful. But Marci is burning up. She's so sick."

"Okay, let's see if we can make it to the hospital."

Gil turned the truck back onto the road, but seconds later he slowed to a stop. "My gosh, look at that. The bridge is washed out from the floodwaters. If that strange man hadn't warned us, we might not have been able to stop in time. We would have driven right into the water and drowned!"

"We have to go back," said Lindy. "We have no choice."

"It looks like we're on our own," declared Lindy once they returned home and put Marci back to bed. Lindy took her daughter's temperature. "Oh, dear, her fever is now 103.4."

"Let's keep putting cold washcloths on her face to cool her down," Gil suggested. "I wish the doctor were here."

"We'd better stay with her the rest of the night," said Lindy. "We'll take turns watching over her. I'll take the first shift, and then you take over at four A.M."

Lindy sat in a chair next to the bed, turned on the light, and read out loud to Marci, who kept moaning and coughing. Eventually the little girl fell asleep. Lindy put down Marci's book and picked up a novel. She read until about 3:30 A.M., then dozed off.

About 15 minutes later Marci woke up and felt a cool hand on her blazing-hot forehead. It was a soft big hand gently caressing her head. Marci fluttered her eyes open, expecting to see her mother or dad. To her surprise, she saw it was the man in the white coat.

Just as Marci was about to scream, he smiled and put his index finger to his lips, indicating to her to remain quiet. The little girl exhaled. There was a manner about the stranger that made Marci feel relaxed rather than scared.

From the bedside light Marci saw the elderly man's face much clearer now. His dark brown eyes gleamed with compassion. Short bristles of gray hair covered the top of his pale round face. The wrinkles around his eyes and mouth spread out in such a way that it looked to Marci as though the man laughed and smiled a lot. His white coat was open, revealing a dark blue suit over a white shirt and neatly knotted red striped tie.

"Who are you?" Marci whispered.

The man said nothing. He stepped back, cocked his head, and folded his arms as if he were in deep thought. All the while he kept staring at her with those kindly eyes.

Marci looked over at her mother, who was still snoozing

in the chair next to the bed. "Mommy," Marci whispered. "Mommy, wake up. There's somebody here. The man in white."

Lindy woke up but didn't see anyone else in the room. "Huh? What? Where is he?" she sputtered with alarm.

Marci pointed to the other side of the bed and said, "He was right there a second ago. He stood there and stared at me—and I wasn't dreaming either. You do believe me, don't you?"

"I don't know what to believe." Lindy felt her daughter's forehead and took her temperature. It had continued to climb. "All I know is that you are still very sick."

Lindy went into the next bedroom and woke up her husband. "It's almost four o'clock, Gil."

"How's Marci?"

"Not well. Her temperature is 104. And she claims she saw the man in white again in her room. What do you make of that?"

"At first I assumed the man was someone she saw in her mind because of her high fever. But we saw him in the road. The way he appears and disappears, it's as if he's a ghost."

"Maybe he is, but I can't concern myself with him now," said Lindy. "It's Marci I'm worried about. I feel so helpless. I wish there was something more we could do for her. Will you watch her now while I get some sleep?"

Gil walked into Marci's bedroom and kept a vigil while she fitfully tossed and turned. At daybreak he looked out the window and counted at least five fallen trees. One of them had ripped down the power lines to the house. *Things couldn't get much worse,* Gil thought. *The power is cut, our phone is dead, the bridge is washed out, and our little girl is very ill. We need help.*

He walked into the kitchen and turned on the gas stove to boil water for tea. *Well, at least something works around here.* As he waited for the kettle to boil, he sat down at the kitchen table, put his head in his hands, and tried to figure out what to do for Marci. When the kettle began to whistle, he got up. To his astonishment, he saw the man in white standing on the opposite side of the room.

"It's you!" shouted Gil. "Who are you? What do you want? Why do you keep appearing and disappearing?"

The old man smiled and held up his hand to quiet Gil. Without saying a word, the man gestured for Gil to follow him. It didn't make any sense for Gil to let a complete stranger in the house without knowing more about him. But Gil had a gut feeling that this man—or ghost—was no threat to him or his family.

The man walked silently into the den with Gil at his heels. He motioned to the floor-to-ceiling bookcase that had been built into the wall. "That's my bookcase," said Gil. "What about it?"

The man pointed to a particular shelf and indicated to Gil to remove the books there. Once the shelf was cleared, the man motioned him to push on the back panel. Gil did and found that the panel pivoted open, revealing a secret little hideaway.

"Why, I never knew this was here!" exclaimed Gil. "How did you know?"

The man acted slightly impatient and gestured for him to reach inside the compartment. Gil pulled out a small leather case. He opened it up and looked inside. "It's a doctor's bag," said Gil. "It's got medicine and needles inside." He turned to the man and said, "You're a doctor, aren't you? That explains the white coat. You knew these medical supplies were hidden here." The man nodded.

Gil didn't ask why the man wouldn't speak. Instead, Gil did as he was told through the man's hand gestures. After Gil emptied the bag, the man pointed to a syringe and a vial—a small sealed glass tube filled with a clear liquid labeled amoxicillan.

"That's an antibiotic, isn't it?" asked Gil. The man nodded and then, without touching anything, pretended to give himself an injection in his hip.

"Wait a second," Gil said warily. "You want me to fill the syringe with this medicine and then give a shot to my daughter? I don't know about that. I don't want to play around with Marci's life."

The man clasped his hands together and wordlessly pleaded with him to give Marci the injection. Gil stared at the stranger and wondered what to do. "My daughter is getting sicker, and we're trapped in this house. I can't explain it, but I trust you. This is all so strange, but I'm desperate enough to do anything to help Marci."

Heeding the man's unspoken advice, Gil went upstairs with him to Marci's room, where she was still sleeping. Gil filled the syringe, took a deep breath, and murmured, "Oh, I hope I'm doing the right thing." He gave Marci the shot, but she was so sick it didn't wake her.

"Okay, I did it," Gil said, turning around. "Hey, where did you go?"

"I'm right here, honey," said Lindy as she stepped into the bedroom.

"No, I mean the man in white. He was right here."

"You saw him here? Then where is he? He's not in the room, and I just came from the hallway." She suddenly noticed that Gil was holding a syringe in his hand. "My gosh, Gil, what are you doing with that needle? You're not a doctor or a nurse. Tell me you didn't give her a shot."

When Gil explained what had happened, Lindy broke down and cried. "Some stranger who doesn't say a word comes into our house and tells you to give our daughter an injection of something you think is an antibiotic and you do it? Are you out of your mind?"

"I was frantic, and I had a gut feeling that this man or ghost—or whoever he was—came here to help."

Lindy raced downstairs and found the doctor's bag in the den and the secret hideaway in the bookshelf. When she returned, Marci was still sleeping. "Sweetie, please get better, please," Lindy whispered, stroking the child's head.

Two hours later Marci began to stir and opened her eyes. "Hi, Mommy."

"How do you feel?"

"Much better."

Lindy felt Marci's forehead. "Your fever feels like it's almost gone!" After taking her temperature, Lindy declared, "Your fever has definitely broken—99.8! That's fantastic! Maybe the doctor's medicine worked after all!"

"Is that the doctor who gave me the medicine?" asked Marci, pointing to a spot behind her mother. Lindy turned around and gasped. Leaning against the doorway was the man in white. He smiled, bent at the waist ever so slightly, and then slowly vanished right before their eyes.

"Mommy did you see that? He just disappeared."

"I saw it, but I don't believe it."

Lindy raced out into the hallway and then went into every room in the house without finding him. She dashed into her bedroom and woke up Gil. "We saw him! The man in white was in Marci's bedroom, and then he disappeared into thin air!"

"How's Marci?"

"Gil, her fever broke! She feels so much better. I think she's going to be okay!"

When the stormed died down, the Dunlaps took Marci to her regular physician, Dr. Gerald Smythe, who discovered that she had been suffering from pneumonia. Without going into any details, they told him that a houseguest of theirs was a doctor who had injected her with an antibiotic.

"It's a good thing the physician was visiting," said Dr. Smythe. "If he hadn't been there, Marci could have died. But now she'll make a complete recovery."

Back home Gil and Lindy wanted to solve the mystery man's identity. "The way he came and went without entering or leaving the house can mean only one thing," said Lindy. "That man was a ghost."

"It's the only explanation," agreed Gil. "That would explain why he didn't appear wet out in the storm."

"He saved our lives by warning us about the bridge. And he saved Marci's life with that medication."

"Since he knew where the medical bag was hidden, he

must have lived here," said Gil.

"But when we bought the house two years ago from the Faynes, they never said anything about a doctor living here. I'm going to call them. I think they moved to Montreal."

The phone call solved the mystery. Mrs. Fayne said her father was a doctor who had built the house in the 1950s. When he became a widower in 1988, he became semiretired and gave the house to his newlywed daughter. He lived with her and her husband during the summer and spent the winters in Florida until his death shortly before the house was sold two years ago.

"Mrs. Fayne," Lindy said, "do you know anything about a secret compartment in the bookshelf?"

"Oh, my heavens, yes. I forgot all about it. About ten years ago our house was burglarized. The thieves stole drugs and other medical supplies that my father kept in his home office. So he had the secret compartment built to make sure no one would ever steal drugs from him again."

"Could you describe your father to me?"

"He was tall, about six feet (1.8 m); 180 pounds (82 kg); short, gray hair, round face. He always dressed up in a suit and tie and wore a long white doctor's coat."

"That's the man."

"What do you mean?"

"Oh, nothing, Mrs. Fayne," said Lindy.

"He was a very good doctor," said Mrs. Fayne.

"Believe it or not," said Lindy in a voice cracking with emotion, "he still is."

THE
FIRES OF OCTOBER

Birthdays are happy events for most kids. But for several troubling years, Shawn Mitchell dreaded his. He had good reason. Every year around his birthday, from the age of 10 to 12, terror consumed his life.

The kids at school thought Shawn was one of the luckiest boys around because his dad, Mike, was a sportswriter who covered all the big events—the Super Bowl, the NBA Finals, and the World Series. Shawn knew better. Sure, he was proud of his father and loved all the neat gifts he brought home, such as a bat used by Barry Bonds, a football autographed by Dan Marino, and a basketball jersey worn by Charles Barkley. But his father traveled a lot and was hardly ever home—and never on Shawn's birthday, October 21, because Mike Mitchell was always covering the World Series.

Shawn's 10th birthday was no exception. He had three classmates over to the family's apartment for a small party, which his dad couldn't attend. It wasn't a big party because, although the kids at school seemed to like him, Shawn was pretty much a loner. The Mitchells' only child spent most of his free time reading. He loved sports, but because he was overweight and not very coordinated, he was content to watch rather than play.

A few hours after the party Shawn sat on his bed, aimlessly sorting through his baseball card collection. *Gee, I wish Dad were here,* he thought. *Just once I'd like him not to cover the World Series so he could be home with me. Or maybe one day he could take me to the Series with him. It would be so cool. . . . Hmm, I wonder what that crackling sound is.* He turned his head and, to his shock, saw a line of small flames licking up from the bottom of his bedroom curtains.

"Mom! Come quick! My curtains are on fire!"

His mother, Nancy, rushed in, yanked the curtains from the rod, and stomped out the fire.

"Are you okay?" she asked, catching her breath. Once she knew that Shawn was fine, Nancy looked him in the eye and, in a low tone of voice, said, "Explain how this happened, Shawn."

"Mom, I didn't do anything. I was sitting on my bed, and when I turned around, the curtains were on fire."

"The fire didn't start by itself," said Nancy. "Were you playing with matches?"

"No way," he replied, vigorously shaking his head. "I know better than that. I didn't start the fire—and that's the truth."

"I know you don't lie, Shawn."

"Are you going to tell Dad?"

"Well, of course I am. He'll be relieved to know that you weren't hurt. But he'll also be puzzled over how it started." She examined the windowsill and floor. "We're very lucky.

Nothing else was damaged. The walls aren't even singed. This is so strange."

The next day, while his mother was fixing dinner, Shawn was watching television in the den when he noticed flames reflecting off the TV screen. He jerked his head around and let out a frightened scream. Fist-sized flames were shooting up from the seat of his father's favorite chair. "Mom!" Shawn cried out. "Fire! It's Dad's chair!"

Shawn snatched a cushion off the couch and beat out the small fire. Nancy ran over to him and surveyed the damage—a small charred spot on the chair. Then she gave him a stern look.

"I know what you're going to say, Mom. But I had nothing to do with it. I was just watching TV when I first saw the flames."

Nancy sighed. "Shawn, were you playing with any chemicals or anything that might have accidentally—"

"Mom, I swear it wasn't me."

When Mike came home three days later, he and Nancy had a long talk with Shawn about the fires. Trying to remain calm and understanding, they had their doubts about their son. But with no evidence to the contrary, they accepted his word.

Their faith in their son seemed to pay off. No new fires sprouted in the apartment—that is, until the following year.

The Mitchells had all but forgotten about the blazes. But then, two days after Shawn's father left to cover the World Series—which was right before Shawn's 11th birthday—the freaky fires ignited again. Only this time they included an eerie new twist.

Shawn was reading in his room when he heard a creepy snickering . . . "Heh-heh-heh" . . . like the sinister chuckle of the villain in a cartoon show. Before he had a chance to find the source of the laugh, Shawn was filled with dread. WHOOSH! A circle of flames the size of a dinner plate erupted on the bedspread at his feet. Shawn jumped up, grabbed his pillow, and smothered the fire. "It's happening all over again!" he moaned.

He felt sick to his stomach as he hurried into his parents' room and broke the news to his mother. "This is terrible!" she exclaimed. "I thought we wouldn't ever be bothered by those fires again."

"Why is it happening to me?" asked Shawn, knowing his mother had no answer.

"This can't go on," she declared. "We need to get to the bottom of this immediately."

The next morning, while eating cereal alone in the kitchen, Shawn heard that same scary laugh coming from out of nowhere.

"Heh-heh-heh."

Shawn dropped his spoon and yelled out, "Mom! There's going to be another fire!" He grabbed a fire extinguisher from the closet and paced the kitchen floor. His skin crawled with worry as he waited helplessly for the next flare-up. Seconds later his fear was realized. A spot on the floor burst into flames. Shawn quickly extinguished it just as his mother hurried into the room.

"What happened?" she asked.

"The floor burst into flames."

"How did you know it would do that?"

"I heard a weird laugh right before the fire," he told her. "It was the same one I heard last night."

Nancy hugged her son and began to cry. "Oh, Shawn, we need to get you some help."

"Me?" he snapped, pushing her away from him. "It's not me who's starting these fires."

"But they only happen when you're in the room alone. What else am I supposed to think?"

"That I'm telling the truth."

"Shawn, I can't bear to see you so troubled," she said. "We must try to get you help. It's for your own good."

"I didn't do it!" he hissed through clenched teeth. He stormed off to his room and slammed the door.

Later that morning Shawn overheard his mother making an appointment for him with a psychiatrist. Shawn was upset that she didn't believe him—and he was worried about when and where the next fire would strike.

That evening Shawn was walking down the hall when he heard the ominous "Heh-heh-heh." That horrible menacing chortle caused Shawn to cringe in panic. "Mom!" Shawn yelled. "Watch out for another fire!" He snatched an extinguisher and scurried around the apartment, searching for the next blaze.

"Oh, no!" shouted Nancy. "Where? Where?"

The two of them made a frantic hunt, but saw no fire. Finally Nancy turned to Shawn and said, "Maybe there won't be a fire this time."

"Yes, there will," he declared. "I heard that same awful laugh that always happens before a fire breaks out."

Nancy's eyes grew big and her mouth opened in shock.

"What?" Shawn demanded. "You think I'm crazy?"

His mother shook her head and pointed over his shoulder. Shawn spun around. "Oh, my gosh!" he shouted. "It's the coffee table!" Flames were shooting out from the tabletop. He rushed over and doused them.

"I'm astounded," said his shell-shocked mom, examining the small burn mark on the table. "I saw the fire start on its own."

"Now do you believe me?" asked Shawn. "Now do you understand that I couldn't possibly have done it?"

His mother bent over and kissed his forehead. "Yes, Shawn, I believe you didn't start any of the fires." She hugged him. "I'm sorry for ever doubting you." But then she began to tremble once she realized that the cause of the fires remained unexplained.

As tears welled in his eyes, Shawn asked, "Mom, why are these fires bursting out in our home?"

"I don't know, honey. I simply don't know. But we're not spending another night in our apartment until this mystery is cleared up."

A fire inspector examined the scene of the small flare-ups. "This is the darnedest thing I've ever seen," he told them. "I can't find any cause for these fires. There's no smoke residue, no ash, no odor, and very little damage in the burn area."

Shawn had a terrible feeling that he was connected to the fires. All of them occurred in his presence—and around the time of his birthday. Just as unsettling was the fact that only he heard that terrible snickering.

When Shawn's dad returned home, he brought in another

fire expert to carefully check the apartment in an effort to find the cause of the puzzling blazes. The expert examined the floors and walls and every wire, electrical outlet, knickknack, and piece of furniture. He left scratching his head.

Another year passed without any more fires. But as October rolled around, Shawn became increasingly edgy. He knew those blazes would start up again. If only he understood why . . . if only he understood how to stop them.

"Dad, do you have to cover the Series this year?" Shawn asked. "Couldn't you stay home in case those fires come back? At least you'd be here for my birthday."

"Son, I'd love to stay. But you've heard me tell Mom how I don't get along with my boss. He won't let me take the time off. He's looking for any excuse to get me fired, so if I back out now, I'll likely lose my job."

The night before his 12th birthday, Shawn sank into a depression. He felt sad that his father wasn't home and scared that at any moment he would hear that unearthly snicker. He didn't have to wait long.

Shawn was in the bathroom, brushing his teeth before bed and feeling sorry for himself. Suddenly he saw a sight that sent shock waves rippling through his body. A small ball of gray smoke began swirling near the ceiling. With every turn the curls of smoke grew thicker, darker, and larger. They dropped lower and lower until they transformed into a man-sized cloud.

Shawn watched frozen in terror as the billowing cloud burst forth with a bloodcurdling laugh that left the boy weak-kneed from fright. Seconds later the cloud withered away. Then . . . WHOOSH! Three-foot- (1-m-) tall flames sprang up from the middle of the bathtub. Recovering from his horror, Shawn turned on the faucet and drowned the fire.

Exhausted from the terror, Shawn told his mother about the menacing cloud. "Mom, I think an evil ghost is causing these fires. We've got to find a way to get rid of it."

When Nancy Mitchell phoned her husband to tell him what happened, Mike Mitchell ordered his family to leave their home immediately until he returned. They stayed with relatives for the next several days while authorities again combed the apartment. But no one found a clue to the cause of the mysterious fires.

In desperation the Mitchells brought in a psychic investigator, Dr. Karl Schmidt. After spending several hours alone in the apartment, Dr. Schmidt told the Mitchells what they didn't really want to hear: "I detected the presence of a troubled ghost. Since these strange fires happen in October around Shawn's birthday, there might be a link between the boy and the ghost."

Dr. Schmidt then asked Shawn, "Can you remember how you were feeling during the minutes before the fires started?"

"Sad, depressed, lonely," Shawn replied.

"Why?"

"Because my dad's gone a lot, and he's never home for my birthday."

After a lengthy chat with Shawn, Dr. Schmidt told the Mitchells, "I have a hunch about what's going on here. Every October Shawn is particularly upset and hurt that Mike is always out of town on his birthday. Shawn gets into a depressed state and somehow—beyond our understanding— a reckless ghost tunes into Shawn's emotions. The ghost is probably a spirit of someone who had a fascination with fire. Feeding off Shawn's depression and loneliness, the ghost starts fires to gain attention and act on some sort of unresolved conflict. Judging from the size of the fires, the ghost isn't out to cause any real damage."

"Except to our minds," declared Nancy.

"How do we make it go away?" Shawn asked.

"The best way is to deny the spirit what it needs to cause the mischief—those powerful emotions of loneliness and sadness."

Mike didn't know whether or not to believe Dr. Schmidt. But he was sure of one thing. He would never miss another one of Shawn's birthdays.

Over the next year no more fires erupted in the Mitchells' apartment. But even better news for Shawn was that his dad took a desk job in the sports department. Although it was for less money, it allowed him to spend more time at home because it required no traveling. Shawn couldn't have been happier. From then on, father and son enjoyed fun outings together, going to football games, the movies, and baseball card shows.

For the first time in years, Shawn actually looked forward to his next birthday because this time his dad would be there with him.

However, as the day of his party drew near, Shawn was worried that the ghostly fire bug would return. But the only flames that flickered on his birthday were the ones from the 13 candles on his cake.

THE HAUNTING
OF 707 HIGHVIEW

The Burton family never believed in ghosts—that is, until they moved into the old Victorian house at 707 Highview.

The stately 12-room, three-story house was built at the turn of the century. It featured 14-foot (4-m) ceilings, oak floors, ornate moldings, four fireplaces, and six stained-glass windows. Although the place needed renovating, the Burtons fell in love with it at first sight. Raymond and Mary Burton were antique dealers who appreciated the authentic detailing and workmanship of the house.

Before moving in, they had replaced the wiring and plumbing and installed central air-conditioning and a new furnace. Tragically, the old furnace had proved deadly. A year earlier a valve had rusted out, causing carbon monoxide to build up and escape. The colorless, odorless, lethal gas seeped into the bedrooms of Harold and Ethel Gaylord, the previous owners of the house, and killed them.

During their first night in the house, Raymond and Mary,

along with their children Paul, 15, Hannah, 13, and Leah, 11, were eating Chinese takeout food in the kitchen and discussing the former owners.

"Paul and I learned a lot about the Gaylords from the neighbors across the street," Hannah reported. "Harold and Ethel were brother and sister who never married. They inherited the house from their parents and lived here for the last 50 years or so—and they hated anything new."

"Yeah," said Paul. "They were stuck in their old ways. Harold mowed the yard with an old hand pushmower. They used rotary phones instead of touch-tone. They wouldn't dream of having a microwave or a stereo or a dishwasher. And, get this, they never owned a TV set! Can you believe it?"

"No TV?" said Leah. "How can you live without TV?"

Paul took a bite of food and continued, "Did you know that up until the time of their death, they still drove the same car they had for 40 years—a 1954 Chevrolet? It was so old it became an antique. But they kept it in excellent condition. In fact, after their death it was worth thousands more than what they paid for it new."

Hannah nodded and added, "They hardly ever drove anywhere except to the movies, and they stopped doing that years ago because they said movies were getting too disturbing.

"The Gaylords' only modern device was an old cabinet radio. They would spend hours listening to big-band and classical music. Otherwise, they didn't want to change. The neighbors said it was like having a living museum on the block. The Gaylords always talked about the good old days. The problem was they refused to leave them. They were afraid of today's world and wanted everything to stay the same as it used to be."

"And get a load of this," said Paul. "When they died, they left two hundred thousand dollars in the bank! They could have afforded the best of everything—fancy car, wide-screen TV, new appliances, everything that would have made life more comfortable for them. But they were stuck in their old ways. That's why they didn't modernize the house."

"Well," said their father, "we'll keep the house's charm, but this old house will undergo a great many changes by the time we get through with it."

Just then the ornate crystal chandelier above the dining-room table began to shake ever so slightly, creating an eerie tinkling sound.

"Wow!" Hannah exclaimed. "Look at that!"

"Kind of spooky," murmured Leah.

"You don't suppose this place is haunted, do you?" Paul teased.

"Don't be silly," Mary replied. "It's probably caused by the vibration from the traffic outside."

"Could be," said Paul. "But the timing was pretty incredible. Maybe the ghosts of Harold and Ethel are giving us a welcome."

Actually, as the Burtons would soon discover, it was quite the contrary.

The next day proved frustrating while the Burton family began remodeling the living room. Tools kept disappearing.

"Hey, where's the tape measure?" asked Hannah. "I had it here just a second ago."

"Has anyone seen my hammer?" asked Paul. "I set it down on the floor."

"Okay, who's playing games?" Raymond demanded. "Leah, are you hiding things?"

"Hey, don't blame me, Daddy," she replied. "I can't find the screwdriver."

That night Hannah stepped in the shower, turned it on, and reached for the soap. Instead of touching the soap, she felt a palm-sized square metal object in her hand. To her surprise, it was the tape measure. Across the hallway Leah pulled down the covers of her bed and found the screwdriver. Meanwhile, when Paul went into the closet to hang up his clothes, he stubbed his toe on the missing hammer.

When the kids reported their discoveries to their parents, Raymond asked, "Can you think of any rational explanation for why the missing items would turn up in the shower, bed, and closet?"

No one could.

The next day the Burtons began stripping the old wallpaper off the walls. They hauled in buckets of hot water in which they dipped sponges and then soaked the paper to help make scraping easier.

"This wallpaper is ugly!" Leah declared.

Suddenly one of the buckets of hot water tipped over, splashing her. "Yeow! That's hot!" Everyone looked at her. "Hey, it wasn't me," said Leah. "I wasn't that close to the bucket."

"Well, it certainly wasn't any of us," said Raymond.

"I didn't touch it," Leah claimed. "It tipped over by itself." But no one really believed her.

While stripping a wall, Hannah removed a big piece of old wallpaper and made an unexpected discovery. "There's writing underneath this stuff," she announced. Scrawled on the wall in brush strokes of red were the letters *V* and *E* two feet (61 cm) high. "Maybe there are more letters underneath," she said. The Burtons scraped cautiously to find out what else was hidden behind the old wallpaper. Once they had stripped the wall, they stood back to read the message and were bewildered by it:

LEAVE US ALONE!

"What do you suppose it means?" asked Hannah.

"These must have been troubled people," replied her father. "Maybe sometime way back the Gaylords didn't want to be bothered and let others know it by painting a message on the wall."

"The way it's written gives me the creeps," said Leah.

"Say, is it just me or is it awfully hot in here?" asked Paul. He walked over to the thermostat and said, "No wonder. It's set at ninety-eight degrees."

The Burtons looked at one another. No one had touched it except Mary, who had set the temperature at 72 the previous day after the thermostat unexplainably had been set at a chilly 58.

That evening Raymond finished installing his electric treadmill, which he had used in their previous house. He set the machine at the usual speed and began walking briskly. Soon the treadmill sped up on its own. As Raymond reached for the control knob, the treadmill kicked into racing speed and propelled him backward. He lost his footing and was thrown off the machine, slamming into the dresser with a thud. He scrambled to his feet, turned off the machine, and then sat on the edge of the bed, rubbing his back and wondering what went wrong.

Meanwhile, Mary was sitting in the living room reading a magazine when she felt a drop of water on her head. More splats followed. She looked up and saw water dripping from the ceiling. *Oh, no. Don't tell me a water pipe is leaking,* she thought. Mary ran upstairs and into her bathroom. Water was gushing out of the tub faucet and overflowing the sides, leaving an inch of water on the floor.

After turning off the faucet, she asked Raymond, "Did you turn on the bathwater and forget about it?"

"No," he replied. "I heard the water running, but I thought you were taking a bath."

"Just another weird occurrence in this old house," Mary muttered as she began sopping up the wet floor with towels.

Getting increasingly irritated and mystified by the string of annoyances, the Burtons were not prepared for the shocking surprise that awaited them the next morning. They were looking forward to their first big Sunday breakfast in their remodeled kitchen, which had new top-of-the-line appliances.

Early that morning Mary and Raymond sleepily walked downstairs toward the kitchen, expecting to have their coffee already brewed in the automatic coffeepot. What they saw in the kitchen woke them up in a hurry.

"Oh, Ray, look at this!" Mary cried out. The glass coffeepot had split in two and all the brewed coffee had spilled off the counter and trickled onto the floor.

"How long before this streak of bad luck ends?" she wondered. Not soon enough, as they discovered after the kids entered the kitchen and pitched in to clean up the spill and help cook breakfast.

Leah took sausage out of the freezer, stuck it into the microwave, and set the timer for two minutes.

"Hannah, how about setting the table?" asked Mary. "The clean dishes are in the dishwasher."

As Hannah pulled out the dishes, she said, "They didn't get cleaned, Mom."

"What?" Mary walked over to her and examined the dirty dishes. "I filled the dishwasher last night, put the soap in it, and started it," Mary recalled. "I even remember telling Dad how quiet it sounded. This is very disappointing. We'll have to call the appliance man."

"Hey, Mom, what's that smell?" asked Paul. "It's like burnt toast."

Mary looked around and spotted smoke belching from her favorite appliance. "My bread maker!" She rushed over and turned it off. "That's never happened before. Oh, my bread is ruined. I had my heart set on serving homemade bread with apple butter this morning."

"Let's have pancakes instead," Raymond suggested. He poured milk and pancake mix into a blender, put on the top, and turned it on. It whirred for a few seconds, then unexpectedly the top flew off. Pancake batter shot out of the blender, spraying Raymond and Hannah and splattering the walls while everyone screamed and ducked. Shielding her eyes, Hannah dodged through the flying batter and shut off the blender.

"Oh, what a mess!" cried Mary, looking at sticky pancake mix oozing down the walls and counter.

As they started cleaning up, Leah shouted, "The sausage!" She turned off the microwave and pulled out a plate of black shriveled sausage patties.

"Man, you nuked the patties, Leah," said Paul.

"But I set the timer for only two minutes."

"Yeah, well, it had to be going for at least five minutes to char them like that," he said.

"What a great way to start the day," muttered Mary, wiping batter out of her hair.

Raymond leaned over the counter, gazed at his family, and asked, "Anyone want to go to McDonald's for breakfast?"

That night, while Mary and Raymond were visiting neighbors, the kids experienced their most bizarre moments yet in the old house.

Hannah finished hooking up her stereo receiver and tuned in to her favorite rock station. She was listening to a rock song when suddenly a classical piece by Bach blared over her speakers. She walked over to the tuner and saw that it had moved to a classic music station. Wondering how that could have happened, she turned back to the rock channel. But minutes later the radio was playing classical music again. *This is crazy,* she thought. *Why isn't the rock station signal holding? I'll have to work on the tuner in the morning.* She turned off the radio.

As she lay on top of her bed, she began to hear faint music. *Am I hearing classical music again? It must be in my head. No, it's getting louder. Maybe Paul's room?* She got out of bed and made a startling discovery. *Why, it's coming from my radio! But I turned it off. How could it have turned on by itself? Must be an electrical short.* She pulled the cord out of the wall, and the music stopped.

Then Hannah walked downstairs, where Leah was channel surfing on their new wide-screen TV. "I'm trying to learn where all the stations are on the new cable," said Leah. "But something's not right. There's interference on all the stations."

"I can barely make it out. It looks like the fuzzy images of two heads," said Hannah.

Leah nodded and said, "They give me the creeps."

The images slowly turned into better focus until the girls saw the heads of two elderly people—a man and a woman. The wrinkled face of a gray-haired woman looked distressed. Her eyes flashed angrily, and her lips were puckered as if she had sucked on a lemon. The man's eyes squinted, and his mouth angled into a nasty sneer.

Hannah walked up to the screen for a better look and experienced an unsettling feeling. She backed away and then shuddered. "Look!" gulped Hannah. "Their eyes are following me around the room!" She walked to the right of the TV set and then scurried over to the left side. The heads turned with her. "It's like they're real!"

"And in this house!" Leah squealed in fright.

Meanwhile, upstairs Paul was on his computer doing a report about civil-rights leader Dr. Martin Luther King. From a book in his lap he had copied part of one of Dr. King's most memorable speeches and was proofreading it on the screen: "I have a dream that one day GETOUTNOW on the red hills of Georgia, the sons of former slaves and the sons of former slave owners GETOUTNOW will be able to sit together at the table of brotherhood . . ."

Paul was dumbfounded when he looked at his screen. *GETOUTNOW? What's that? How did those words—whatever they mean—get in there? I didn't type that. GETOUTNOW? Wait a second, if I add spaces between some of the letters, they spell GET OUT NOW. What the—?*

Suddenly new text streaked across the screen on its own without Paul touching the keys. Line after line read:

GETOUTNOWGETOUTNOWGETOUTNOW
GETOUTNOWGETOUTNOWGETOUTNOW

My computer is going nuts! Paul hit the Escape key, then the Return key, but nothing worked. Finally in frustration, he turned off the computer. He turned it back on. But when he went to call up his report, it wasn't there, because in his haste, he forgot to save it. Paul waited to see if the computer was going to continue writing the strange message on its own, but it didn't.

It must be some kind of weird computer glitch—or is it really telling me to get out now? Before he had time to think any more about it, he was interrupted by a scream.

"Paul!" yelled Hannah from downstairs. "Come look at the TV!" He could tell from the frightened tone in her voice that there was a problem.

He scampered down the stairs and found Leah and Hannah standing behind the couch, fearfully pointing to the TV. "Those faces are staring at us. They follow us around the room!" said Hannah.

"I'm scared to go near it," said Leah.

"What is this, a joke?" he asked. But the alarmed look in his sisters' eyes convinced him otherwise. And so did the fact that the heads in the TV screen eerily followed him around the room. Feeling goose bumps spring up on his arms, Paul hurried behind the set and pulled the plug. The picture darkened immediately—but the images lingered for several seconds before slowly fading away.

When Mary and Raymond returned home, the anxious kids told them what had happened. It was time for a family conference.

"It's obvious that this house has a life of its own," said Raymond. "We can try to blame some of these things on faulty wiring, cable problems, what have you. But the truth is all our appliances, electronics, and plumbing should work fine. I'm beginning to believe that the strange things in this house are caused by forces that are beyond our understanding."

"Dad, do you think this house is haunted?" asked Paul.

Raymond sighed and nodded. "As silly as it sounds, yes, I do."

"Me too," admitted Mary.

"Do you think the ghosts are Harold and Ethel Gaylord?" asked Hannah.

"Kids, I have something to show you." Raymond held up two framed photos—one of a ruddy-faced middle-aged man with short-cropped hair and the other of a middle-aged frumpy woman with short tightly curled hair. "Now, picture in your mind what they'd look like 30 years later. Do you recognize them?"

"They're the faces we saw on the TV screen!" declared Hannah.

Both Paul and Leah agreed. "Ooh, they give me the shivers," said Leah.

"I thought you'd recognize them," said Raymond. "I found these photos in the attic. According to the writing on the back, they're photos of Harold and Ethel taken in 1962."

"That clinches it," said Paul. "They're the ghosts haunting this house!"

"Why are they harassing us?" asked Hannah.

"Well," said Raymond, "we learned that Harold and Ethel hated change and wanted everything to stay the same in their lives. I think that's what their ghosts are saying to us. Remember all the crazy things that happened the first day we moved in, how our tools disappeared and then reappeared in the oddest places?"

"And we saw that scary message 'Leave us alone' behind the wallpaper," added Leah. "And the water bucket tipped over, and the thermostat acted goofy."

"Right," said Raymond. "We also learned how Harold and Ethel hated new technology."

"Yes," said Hannah. "We learned the hard way, especially in the kitchen."

"And on my computer and your stereo and our television," added Paul.

"The spirits of Harold and Ethel obviously don't like all the changes in the house," said Raymond. "I'm afraid they'll continue to bother us unless we take action right now. We certainly can't live this way."

"What can we do to make them stop?" asked Leah.

"Maybe we need to make them feel more comfortable with things that brought them joy," said Raymond.

"Like what?" asked Mary.

Raymond held up a videocassette and several CDs. "They loved to go to the movies. So I went to the video store and rented an old classic for us to watch—*It Happened One Night*. It's a comedy starring Clark Gable, who was a superstar way back then. Maybe the Gaylords will watch it with us and enjoy it. I also bought some CDs of the big-band sound and other music from their era that I thought they'd appreciate."

"What a minute, Dad," said Hannah. "Are you going to use modern inventions to calm ghosts who are upset because we use modern inventions?"

Raymond grinned and nodded. "It's worth a try. I just hope the Gaylord ghosts like them enough to stop the mischief."

From then on, every week, the Burtons would rent a video of a classic film. The kids complained at first because the movies seemed hokey, but eventually they learned to enjoy them.

Also, every so often during the day, the Burtons played a CD of music from the twenties, thirties, or forties. They usually put the CD on when everyone was heading out of the house, because no one was fond of that kind of music.

But apparently the ghosts of Harold and Ethel Gaylord appreciated the videos and CDs, because the Burtons never saw or were bothered by the phantoms again.

However, every once in a while Hannah would find the tuner on her stereo mysteriously set on the classical music station.

THE CRYING CAVE

For years no one knew the cave even existed. It was just an old cavern carved out of limestone near the bottom of a sheer ravine. It wasn't much different from hundreds of others in the area except for one thing—every so often someone would hear the spooky sounds of wailing echoing from the inside.

That's why they called it the Crying Cave.

It probably never would have been discovered if it hadn't been for Jill Montgomery and Zeke Holland. They were the 16-year-olds who found it by accident—and unlocked a creepy secret that nearly cost them their lives.

The couple were hiking through the hills of western Pennsylvania one Saturday when a heavy downpour hit the area. They pulled rain gear out of their backpacks and decided to head for their car three miles (4.8 km) away.

But Zeke, who was leading the way, slipped on a narrow muddy trail that snaked along the edge of a steep ridge. As he slid down the embankment, he grabbed a bush that was sticking out of the side. However, the roots, weakened by the rain, gave way, causing a section of the trail under Jill to collapse. Both Zeke and Jill tumbled down the muddy ridge and crashed into the bottom of a ravine where a stream was beginning to swell from the heavy rains.

"My back," moaned Zeke. "I think I've sprained it."

"My hip hurts," Jill complained. "I smashed it against a rock when we slid down the hill."

"This isn't good. We're in the middle of nowhere, and no one knows we're here. It's cold and wet and muddy. We're both hurt, and we're a couple of miles from our car. What else can go wrong?"

RUMBLE. RUMBLE.

Jill looked up and screamed, "Zeke! Look out! That boulder is coming right toward us!"

About 10 feet (3 m) above them, a rock about the size of a small car had toppled off its perch. The teens rolled to the left and out of the way just as the boulder, loosened by the rain, bounded past them and crashed into the rushing stream.

"That was too close for comfort," said Zeke.

"We need to get out of here," Jill declared. "Come on."

"I can't walk very far," he replied. "I'm hurt. I need to rest a bit more."

"Hey, what's that?" she asked, pointing to the spot where the boulder had dislodged.

"It looks like an entrance to a cave!"

"Let's see if we can get up there. That will keep us out of the rain and give us some shelter."

The two slowly climbed up to the opening and cautiously went into the limestone cave. They sat down and caught their breath. "It sure is chilly in here," Jill said. "But at least we're out of the rain. It's really coming down now. How's your back?"

"It hurts—a lot," he answered. "How's your hip?"

"About the same as your back."

"We'll have to stay here until the rain lets up and the pain eases. But we can't wait too long, or our parents will be very worried."

"This place gives me the willies," Jill said with a shiver. "You don't suppose there are any bears or snakes or nasty critters in here, do you?"

"If there are, I hope they're friendly."

"I still feel uneasy. Like we're not alone."

"Let's just rest," Zeke said.

They stretched out on the cave's floor and put their backpacks under their heads. The rushing stream and pounding rain echoed eerily in the cave. But above the natural sounds Zeke heard a faint whimper that slowly increased in pitch. "Jill, it's okay," he whispered soothingly. "We'll get out of here safe and sound. I promise. Don't cry."

Jill turned over and replied, "I'm not crying. In fact, I thought you were crying."

"Me? I don't cry."

"Well, if it wasn't me and it wasn't you, then—"

"Shhhhhhh."

The whimper turned into a wail and grew more anguished.

"It sounds like a man crying," said Jill. "And it's coming from deeper in the cave."

"Maybe it's someone who's lost or hurt."

"Hello!" shouted Jill. "Is anyone back there?"

There was no response, but the mysterious crying stopped as quickly as it had started.

"It was probably an animal," said Zeke. "But we'd better go check, just in case it was a person."

Despite the pain in his back and in her hip, the couple inched their way into the darkening cave. But they soon gave up. "We can't go back any farther," said Jill. "It's too dark, and we don't have a flashlight."

Suddenly both teens felt overcome with a wave of terrible sadness that neither had ever experienced before. It was an overwhelming feeling of despair and heartache.

Tears began streaming down Jill's face. "I feel so sad, so empty," she said.

Zeke's eyes watered. "I do too. But it's not about the fix we're in. I mean, I'm a little worried. But this is big-time sadness over something I can't explain. It's different and so powerful. Why do I feel so badly?"

They slumped to the cave floor and held each other tightly. Neither said a word. Finally the combined effects of their weariness, aches, and emotions left them exhausted, and they dozed off.

Then they began to dream.

A young woman was weeding in a garden of pansies and marigolds. She wore a pink bonnet and a gingham dress and was humming a sweet tune. On the other side of the fence her father and brothers were plowing the fields behind two sweaty draft horses. In the opposite direction, on the porch of their farmhouse, her two sisters were taking turns churning butter.

While hoeing the garden and singing, she was startled by the sight of a strapping young man leaning against the wooden fence rail. "Oh, my," she said, her face blushing. "I didn't realize you were there."

"I'm sorry if I alarmed you," said the young man. "I was passing through and heard that lovely song. You have a beautiful voice."

"Why, thank you," she said, still blushing.

"Please, continue singing."

"Oh, no, no. I couldn't."

Just then her father came over from the fields. "Hello, stranger, can I help you?"

"Hello, I'm just passing through. I recently graduated from Harvard and live in New York City. I was taking a train trip to see relatives in Ohio. But when I got to Philadelphia, I decided to hike the rest of the way so I could meet good people. I've found room and board from folks who have fed me and put me up for the night. I have money and always pay them for their kindness."

"Well, you're welcome to come stay with us," said the father. "There's an extra bed in the cellar house."

"That's mighty fine of you, sir. I'd like to take you up on your hospitality." He then turned and flashed a grin at the pretty girl who smiled back.

Jill woke up, shivering and achy. *Where am I? Why is it so dark?* Then it dawned on her. *Oh, we're still in this cave.* She glanced over to Zeke, who was still sleeping. As she limped over to the cave's entrance, she felt pain and stiffness in her hip. *Ow, it's worse now than it was earlier.* She glanced outside.

The rain was coming down in sheets. But what scared her was the swollen stream. It was now a raging torrent of mud creeping up to within a few feet of the cave's entrance.

"Zeke! Zeke! Wake up!"

"Huh? What is it?"

"We're trapped! The stream is rising. We can't get out!"

Zeke sat up and winced in pain over his bad back. He hobbled to the front of the cave and looked out. "Uh-oh. This is bad—real bad."

"What are we going to do?"

"We can't risk leaving here, Jill. It's too muddy outside. If we slip and fall into that rushing water, we'll drown. Let's gather as many rocks as we can in here and build a dike at the entrance. It won't stop the water from coming in, but it will slow it down. We may have to go farther into the cave and then hope that the rain stops soon and the water goes down."

"We're probably stuck here for the night," said Jill. "Oh, what are our parents going to think? They'll be so worried."

After building a waist-high dike, Zeke took off the bandanna around his neck and secured it to one of the rocks at the entrance. "If there's a search party tomorrow morning, maybe they'll spot it," he said. "There's nothing else we can do now except wait."

They leaned against the damp limestone wall and said nothing for a couple of minutes. Jill finally broke the silence.

"I had this strange dream when I dozed off. It was a long time ago, and I saw a farm where a pretty girl was tending to a garden and singing—"

"—and she was wearing a pink bonnet and a gingham dress?" asked Zeke.

"How could you possibly know that?"

Zeke clutched her arm and said, "The young man walked up and heard her singing, and she stopped—"

"—and the young man said he was a Harvard graduate, and he wanted to meet people."

"Jill, we had the exact same dream!"

"Hush," said Jill. "Do you hear it?"

"It's that eerie crying again."

"It's different this time," she said. "It sounds like a woman in pain."

They hollered toward the back of the cave, but failed to get a response. The whimper slowly grew into a wail of agony.

"This is getting spooky," Zeke declared. "I don't know who's crying or where it's coming from."

"She sounds as if she's in such misery."

Eventually the crying faded away. Night had fallen, throwing the cave into pitch darkness. Although the rain had let up slightly, the stream continued to rise and water began seeping through the dike and into the cave.

"It's so dark," said Jill. "I didn't know black could be this black. I can't see anything. It's so scary."

Once again the exhausted couple dozed off. And once again they dreamed the identical dream.

The handsome stranger enjoyed a nice dinner at the farmhouse and spent most of his time talking to the pretty young woman. Although she didn't say much, she was pleased that he paid her so much attention.

The man told the family that he planned to start law

school in the fall after he returned from his trip. He confessed that he felt a strange force had led him to this particular farm.

Everyone in the family took a shine to him. He went out to the field and hoed rows of corn along with the boys while Pa did the plowing. But everyone could see that he and the young woman liked each other very much. In the evening they would walk down to the creek and share their hopes and thoughts.

The couple fell quickly in love, and two weeks later, the handsome stranger proposed to her by the stream. She threw her arms around him and said yes. That evening he took her father aside and asked for permission to marry his daughter. The father, who had grown to like the young man, thought it was all rather sudden, but gave them his blessing. When the rest of the family was on the porch, the young man announced to them that he was marrying her. He then pulled out a sapphire pendant that dangled from a gold necklace, and he gently placed it around her neck.

He told them he had to go back to New York and make arrangements with his family. He promised to return with his relatives in about two weeks, at which time he would marry his beloved in the little church near the farm.

Every day after he left the young woman went down by the stream, sang songs to herself, and thought of little else but her impending wedding.

"Zeke, are you up?"

"Yeah," he mumbled. "I must have fallen asleep."

"Me too. What time is it?"

He looked at his watch. "About ten P.M. Our parents are probably going crazy with worry."

"The rain has stopped, but now there's a couple of inches of water in the cave. Did you dream anything?"

"Yes," replied Zeke. "The guy and the girl fell in love and got engaged."

"I dreamed it too! Why are we both having this happy dream? Why aren't we having nightmares of being trapped in a cave with a raging river outside? Why do we have these attacks of heartache? And . . . oh, no . . . that awful crying is starting again."

This time it sounded like the anguished weeping of both a man and woman. The cries came in waves. They began low and muffled but grew louder with each passing minute. Then they died down, only to increase in volume again. The woman's moans were punctuated by bursts of pain-racked screams. The man bawled in mournful sobs of sorrow.

One minute Jill and Zeke felt rooted in terror by the constant eerie wailing, and the next moment they were gripped by strange feelings of heartache.

"I don't know how I can feel any worse," muttered Jill. "I'm scared, I'm sad, I'm cold, and I'm hurt."

Zeke became fed up with the cries of misery and yelled, "Stop it! Stop crying!" Then he stumbled in the inky blackness toward the entrance. "I've got to get out of here."

"Zeke, stop! You can't go out there. It's too dangerous. Come back here!"

"Anything's better than listening to this torture."

Finally the crying stopped. The weary teens, on the verge

of cracking from the strain, dozed off again from sheer exhaustion.

The young girl was at the stream admiring her sapphire pendant when a deer bounded in front of her. Before she could appreciate the doe's beauty and grace, a shot rang out and struck her. A hunter who failed to notice the young woman had accidentally shot her. But he didn't know it and ran off after the deer.

Clutching her wound, the woman tried to stagger back to the farm. She made it only a few hundred yards. She stumbled into the cave where she died.

When she didn't return home, the family began a desperate search without success. The next morning her fiancé showed up in a driving rainstorm. When he heard that she was missing, he ran toward the stream where the two had spent so much time together. The stream had turned into a churning swollen river. He came upon the cave and saw a sight that nearly drained the life right out of him.

The love of his life lay dead, her once-pretty dress caked in blood. He picked up her lifeless body and, for hours, held her in his arms and sobbed. He paid no attention to the rising river until it was too late. A flash flood had roared down the valley, and the cave quickly filled up with water. He carried her body and headed deeper into the cave until he could go no farther. He stayed there when all of a sudden a boulder came crashing down and lodged right in front of the cave, blocking the entrance. He lay down her body and tried to push the big rock out of the way. But the force of the floodwaters made it impossible to move.

Meanwhile, the water relentlessly seeped into the cave. When the water level reached his waist, he put his beloved's body up on a ledge and then climbed up there too, with only a two-foot (61-cm) clearance to the ceiling of the cave. The unforgiving water continued to rise. There was nowhere to run or hide or swim. All he could do was hold his lifeless sweetheart in his arms and wait for his own watery death. The water soon reached his chest, then his nose, and then . . .

Jill and Zeke were woken by the rising flood water inside the cave. The teens scrambled to their feet and groped in the darkness, desperately looking for an escape from the water.

With their hands clawing along the sides of the cave, they headed away from the entrance until they reached a dead end. "There's no way out," said Zeke. "We can't go back any farther." They continued to feel their way until they found a ledge. When they scaled it, they both hit their heads on the ceiling of the cave. They had to stay low because the clearance was barely two feet (61 cm).

"This is it, Jill. There's no escape. Either the water goes down or we drown. I'm so sorry I suggested we go hiking."

"Just keep talking to me. Don't go back to sleep."

"I won't, Jill. Since our lives are on the line, there's no way I'm sleeping—unless, of course, it's permanent," he added grimly.

"Zeke, did you have another dream about that couple?"

"Yes! And it looks like we're reliving the last part of it."

"When he holds her dead body and drowns?"

Zeke nodded. "You realize what's happened here, don't you, Jill? The stream outside is where they used to go. This is the cave where they both died. The boulder that fell away from the entrance and nearly hit us was the same one that blocked his escape."

"The cries we've heard are from the ghosts of the couple in our dreams!" said Jill.

"That's right. Somehow, the ghosts have managed to tell us their sad story through our dreams."

"I only hope we get a chance to tell their story again outside this cave. I don't want to end up like them."

By now the water had crept up to the ledge. As they clutched each other tightly, Zeke murmured, "Try to relax. We need to conserve our air."

They huddled silently, wondering if they were going to live or die. The air grew stuffy, and their wet clothes chilled them to the bone as they waited helplessly for nature to decide their fate.

An hour later Zeke shouted with relief, "The water is going down! We're going to make it!"

As fast as it had risen, the water began receding. Soon they could see the faint glow of light coming through between the water and the cave's ceiling.

"I hear someone," Jill said excitedly. "I hear voices!"

From outside the entrance came the booming voice of a rescuer, "Jill! Zeke! Are you in there?"

"You found us!" Jill screamed happily. "We're in here! We're in here!" The teens leaped off the ledge and sloshed in chest-high water toward the front of the cave.

"Stay put!" said the rescuer. "We'll get you out! Are you okay?"

"Cold, tired, and wet but otherwise just fine!" replied Jill.

The search-and-rescue team tied a rope to a small inflatable raft and then tore down the dike and paddled inside the cave. The couple were ready to hop aboard when Zeke said, "Oh, I almost forgot our backpacks. They're up on the ledge. Can I borrow your flashlight?"

The rescuer handed it to him. Zeke climbed up on the ledge and shined the light on his backpack. But then the beam caught something else that left him so shocked he staggered back into the water.

"What is it, Zeke?" asked Jill.

"I just saw a human skull!"

The rescuers climbed onto the ledge and with their flashlights looked for themselves. There in the far corner of the ledge, where the teens had spent the night, the flashlights revealed the skeletons of two humans—one scrunched in the far corner of the ledge with the other draped over it. Around the neck of the prone skeleton was a sapphire pendant on a gold necklace.

An investigation by the medical examiner revealed that the skeletons—a male in his twenties and female in her late teens—were of two people who died sometime in the 1800s. A rifle bullet was found on the ledge underneath the prone skeleton, the remains of a female who had been shot.

"We don't know who they are or what happened to them," the medical examiner told Jill and Zeke.

"We may not know their names," replied Zeke, "but we know exactly what happened to them."

Jill's eyes welled with tears as she added, "Those poor people. I feel so sad for them. Thank goodness our story had a happier ending."

THE
LAST GOOD-BYE

Something is wrong, thought Spud Davis as he shot baskets during the pregame warm-up with his teammates. *Dad should be here by now.*

The 8 P.M. tip-off was only a few minutes away for the conference battle for first place against the arch rival Jefferson High School Knights. Here was Spud, a junior in the varsity's starting lineup for the Central High Panthers in the biggest basketball game of the season, and his father had yet to arrive.

That wasn't like his dad, Reggie Davis, a construction worker whose heart was as big as his 6-foot, 4-inch (1.93-m), 225-pound (102 kg) frame. Reggie, who had never missed a game in the two years that Spud played for Central High, always cheered from the bleachers on the students' side of the gym. He felt he could make more noise there than if he were on the other side where the parents usually sat. The last row, center seat was his spot. Reggie chose that seat because he could stand up and root for his son without blocking the view of anyone behind him. Also, Spud could see him easily from the court.

Reggie Davis was a fixture at both home and away games, applauding the team, shouting encouragement, and yelling at the referees in a booming voice that carried above all the others in the gym. Spud couldn't imagine playing a game without his father in the stands.

Ever since he was big enough to toss a basketball, Spud would spend hours with his dad shooting at the hoop over the garage door. Sometimes at night Reggie would park the car in the driveway and turn on its lights so they could play in the dark. In the winter they shoveled off the snow to clear the way for spirited games of one-on-one.

Spud, who got his nickname from his father because his favorite food was mashed potatoes and gravy, stood only 5 feet, 8 inches (172 cm) tall. But Reggie helped develop the boy's basketball skills until Spud had turned into one of the area's best players.

A single parent, Reggie gained custody of his son after his divorce five years earlier. His boy was the number-one priority in life.

As the pregame shoot-around ended, Spud scanned the stands for his father, but couldn't find him. *I wonder if he's sick*, thought Spud. *He was complaining of a little heartburn at dinner, but he said nothing would stop him from coming. Maybe I have time to phone home.*

Just then the horn sounded, warning both benches that the game was about to start. Spud had a queasy feeling in his stomach, not from facing Jefferson High, but from the thought of playing for the first time without his dad there.

"Davis!" shouted Coach Pollard. "Are you listening to anything I'm saying?"

"Huh? Oh, sorry, Coach."

"Get your head in the game, son!" The coach then went over last-minute instructions before sending his players out onto the court.

Jefferson grabbed a quick lead, scoring the first three baskets, one after a bad pass from Spud. Throughout the first period, Spud stole quick glances at the top row, center seat. But it remained empty. Distracted by his father's absence, Spud made only one of five shots, and at the end of the quarter Jefferson led 18–11.

"Davis!" thundered Coach Pollard. "You're playing like your head is a million miles away. Take a breather on the bench. When you're ready to give me and your teammates 100 percent, let me know." The coach turned to a second-stringer and said, "Jergens, get in for Davis."

Spud sulked at the end of the bench. *C'mon, Spud,* he told himself. *Focus, focus. This is a big game for us, and I'm playing terribly. If only I could stop worrying about Dad.* He looked back up in the stands and searched for his father. *Where is he? Why isn't he here?*

"Davis!" shouted Coach Pollard. "Are you back from wherever your mind had wandered?"

"Yes, sir!" Spud replied, leaping off the bench.

"Then get in there and show me what you can do."

Trying hard to forget about his father, Spud concentrated on the game. He scored a couple of baskets, but didn't play particularly good defense. At the half the Panthers trailed the Knights 34–25.

As the team filed into the locker room, Spud made a quick phone call home, but there was no answer. *Something terrible must have happened,* he thought. *Dad just wouldn't miss this game. Maybe he got into an accident, or maybe it's just car trouble. Yeah, that's probably what happened. He'll be here. He has to show up.*

At the end of halftime Coach Pollard told the team, "Men, we have to shoot better and play tougher defense. We can beat these guys. Remember, it's for first place in the league. One other thing. Jergens, you start the second half in place of Davis. Let's go get 'em, men!"

When they returned to the court, Spud took a deep breath, hoping to spot that familiar smiling face in the back row. But his heart sank when he noticed the seat remained empty.

The Panthers managed to slice four points off the Knights' lead and, with Spud remaining on the bench, trailed at the end of three periods, 49–44. Early in the fourth quarter Jergens picked up his fifth foul and was whistled to the bench.

"Okay, Davis, you've had plenty of time to clear your head," said Coach Pollard. "Now get in there and play basketball!"

Spud took a shot from beyond the foul line but it was blocked. The crowd groaned as Jefferson ran a fast break and scored an easy layup.

As Spud inbounded the ball, he heard a familiar voice bellow from the stands, "Let's go, Spud! You're the man, the go-to man!"

It's Dad! He finally made it here! Spud took a quick peek up into the stands. His heart soared when he spotted his father, standing right where he was supposed to be. Reggie raised his fists above his head and pounded the air just like he always did when he got excited. Spud breathed a sigh of relief . . . until a defender knocked the ball out of his hands and went in for another easy layup. The Panthers now trailed 55–46.

"Davis!" thundered Pollard, slamming his clipboard to the floor in disgust.

"You're the go-to man, Spud!" Reggie shouted.

With his father cheering him on, Spud sparked a furious Panther rally. He nailed a three-point basket. Then he stole the inbounds pass and scored on a layup to close the gap to 55–51 with three minutes left in the game. The Central High fans stomped their feet and roared as Spud made another basket and assisted on two others during the rally. Each time the Panthers scored, he shot his fist into the air and then pointed to his father.

The Panthers trailed 59–57 when they called time-out with only eight seconds left in the game. The crowd was yelling so loudly that the players could hardly hear Coach Pollard. "Get the ball to Davis," he told the team. "It's all up to you, Spud. You've got the hot hand."

As the players broke from the huddle, the noise in the gym rose even higher. But above the din, Spud could hear one distinctive voice: "Spud, you're the man, the go-to man!" There was no way Spud was going to let down his dad or the team.

Spud dribbled the ball, trying to spring free for the shot that could tie the game. "You're the man, Spud! The go-to man!" The fans were shrieking as the final seconds ticked off the clock. *Five . . . four . . . three . . .* Spud faked a shot, getting his defender to jump too soon . . . *two* . . . He eyed the rim . . . *one* . . . Spud fired his shot. With a flick of his wrist he released the ball a heartbeat before the final horn sounded. The ball swished through the net. Spud had tied the score, 59–59!

The crowd erupted in bedlam, shouting and cheering over the clutch shot. But the home fans roared even louder when they saw that the referee had called a foul against Spud's defender. Spud could win the game and be the hero by sinking the free throw.

The Knights called a time-out, hoping that the delay would make Spud tense. He pretended to act cool, but he was so nervous inside he was afraid fans could see his knees shaking.

With Jefferson fans booing and waving their arms, hoping to distract him, Spud stepped to the foul line. He took a deep breath, turned, and looked at his father, who gave him a nod of confidence while shaking his big clenched fists in a show of support. Never before had Spud felt such incredible pressure. Then he remembered what his father had always told him: "When you're really nervous at the foul line, bounce the ball three times, and with each bounce tell yourself, 'I'll make the shot'—and believe it!" Spud followed his father's advice. Then he shot the ball on a pretty arc that swished through the net. The Panthers won the game, 60–59!

The bleachers rocked like never before. Teammates raced up to Spud and pounded him on the back. Cheerleaders and fans spilled onto the court, dancing in celebration. Spud thanked his well-wishers and pushed his way through the crowd to follow through on a ritual he and his dad did after every game, win or lose. Spud ran to the scorer's table and stared up at his father, who remained standing in the last row. First, Spud snapped a salute to his dad, who promptly returned a crisp salute to his son.

Spud grinned and ran into the locker room. After showering, he stepped outside expecting to see his father. But Reggie wasn't there.

Spud asked several parents, including the Millers, if they had seen Reggie. All said they hadn't.

"That's not like him to miss a game," said Mr. Miller.

"It's a shame your dad wasn't here to see your heroics," added Mrs. Miller.

"Oh, he was here," said Spud. "He showed up in the last quarter, cheering from his usual spot."

"In the center seat of the last row?" asked Mr. Miller. "That's strange. We kept looking for him there and never saw him."

Spud searched the hallways and asked other people, but no one had seen Reggie or heard his booming voice during or after the game.

Perplexed, Spud headed back toward the locker room when he saw Officer Jim Barber—a close friend of Reggie Davis's—approach. The cop looked dazed and troubled. "Great game, Spud," Jim mumbled, trying hard to smile.

"Thanks. Say, you haven't seen my dad, have you?"

"Let's go in the locker room," said the officer. "I've got something to tell you."

Spud didn't like the sound of the policeman's voice. Once they walked over to a quiet corner of the room, Spud asked, "What's wrong? Is it Dad? Is he all right?"

126

"Spud, I don't know an easy way to tell you this. Your father passed away this evening."

Spud didn't believe his ears. "Dad is dead?"

"About seven-thirty P.M., Harold Walker showed up to drive him to your game. Reggie started complaining of chest pains, so Harold called 911. By the time the paramedics arrived, Reggie was slumped on the floor, and Harold was giving him CPR. They tried to revive him, but he died on the way to the hospital. There was nothing more they could do for him. We decided to wait and tell you after the game. Spud, I'm so sorry."

Spud shook his head and put his hands over his ears. "I don't want to hear this! It can't be true. Dad was here tonight at the game. He showed up in the fourth quarter and cheered me on. He was standing where he always does—last row, center. So you see, you're wrong. You're wrong!"

Jim grabbed Spud by the shoulders. "Spud, I wish with all my heart I was wrong. But when I heard the call come in over the police scanner, I raced over to your house and arrived within a minute after the paramedics. I went with them to the hospital. He died shortly after eight o'clock."

"But I saw him two hours later," Spud declared. "If it hadn't been for Dad, I never would have played so well in the last quarter. He helped me win the game."

Jim didn't give much weight to what Spud had claimed, assuming that the boy was in denial and in shock. The officer put his arm on Spud's shoulder and said, "If there's anything I can do for you, let me know."

"Thanks. I just need to be alone now." Spud grabbed a basketball, shuffled into the now-empty gym, and dribbled to the foul line where minutes earlier he had won the game. He bounced the ball three times and thought, *If Dad died before the game, that means I saw and heard his spirit even though nobody else did. I guess nothing was going to keep him from missing the game—not even his own death. He came to cheer me one more time and to say good-bye. I love him so much.*

Spud looked up at the empty bleachers and to the spot where Reggie always stood. Then he turned toward the basket and shot the ball. It swished through the net. "That one was for you, Dad."

And for a brief moment he thought he heard those same words that Reggie had shouted so many times before, "You're the man, Spud. You're the go-to man!"